To one of the most intelligent, witty and provocative
commentators in the field of energy issues;
And to one of the most intelligent, witty and
provocative commentators in the field of social
support;
From one of the most intelligent, witty and
provocative commentators in the field of arts
criticism.

February 1988

with thanks for your hospitality, and appreciation
of your good company.

BEHIND
THE
FACADE

By arrangement with BBC Publications,
a division of BBC Enterprises Ltd.

BEHIND
THE
FACADE

STEPHEN GAMES

UNIVERSE BOOKS

New York

Published in the United States of America in 1986
by Universe Books
381 Park Avenue South, New York, NY 10016

86 87 88 89 90 / 10 9 8 7 6 5 4 3 2 1

Printed in the United States of America

Library of Congress Cataloging-in-Publication Data

Games, Stephen.
  Behind the facade.

  Reprint. Originally published: London : Ariel
Books, British Broadcasting Corporation, 1985.
  1. Architecture—Great Britain. 2. Architecture,
Modern—20th century—Great Britain. 3. Architecture—
United States. 4. Architecture, Modern—20th century—
United States. 5. Architects—Influence. I. Title.
NA968.G36 1986   720'.941   86-6956
ISBN 0-87663-650-4

Contents

Acknowledgements

All radio programmes are made in conjunction with producers, and I have been very well served by mine. *What Revival?* and *Digging Graves* were produced by Louise Purslow, to whom I am especially grateful. *A Magnificent Catastrophe, The Best Hated Architect in the World* and *Walter Gropius's Crystal Visions* were produced by Thomas Sutcliffe. Judith Bumpus produced *Sir Edwin Lutyens: The Empire Strikes Back* and *The Reversible Mackintosh.* And Julian Brown produced *Sound Unsound.* On all these programmes, I was given constant encouragement by George Fischer, Head of BBC Radio's Talks and Documentaries Department.

I am of course also grateful to all the speakers who contributed to the original programmes and who are quoted here. The programmes were as much a reflection of their ideas and opinions as of my own.

As far as the making of this book is concerned, I am indebted to Patrick Ducker for showing me how to use a word processor, and then letting me use one; to the staff at the RIBA Library, and at the BBC Reference Library, for their considerable assistance; and to Asher Rozenberg who helped with the proof reading and made numerous valuable suggestions.

Introduction

There is a short story by Jorge Luis Borges in which a young Uruguayan, paralysed after being thrown from a horse, develops a prodigious memory. Among his achievements, he invents an alternative numbering system which involves giving a unique name to each number from one to twenty-four thousand. Seven thousand and thirteen he calls *Máximo Pérez*; seven thousand and fourteen becomes *The Railroad*. It fails to occur to him, however, that in repudiating the systematic repetitions of hundreds, tens and units, he is doing the opposite of counting; he is introducing incoherence.

Television is like the paralysed Uruguayan. It observes a lot of things and gives them all names, without necessarily bringing any coherence to them. In this way it is inescapably concrete, materialistic, perhaps even small-minded. Radio is different. Radio cannot name things because there are no *things* on radio to name. For a thing to exist, it has to be seen. So the problem for radio is that the thing under discussion is always absent, and can only be implied from the discussion which goes on around it. Like ripples on a pond, one has to assume the existence of a cast stone.

The dematerialisation of the object by radio can be a limitation. In programmes about architecture, it is impossible to give a pictorial sense of the building, or convey the subtleties which distinguish similar buildings of different quality. Or at least, if it isn't impossible, it's very tedious. This dematerialisation forces radio to classify and relate, unlike paralysed Uruguayans and television, which only isolate. Radio has to observe more closely, to translate what it has seen into language, and then make it mean something. In this way, while television particularises, radio generalises. It is therefore more loaded in the ideas it discusses.

Ideas are shy creatures. However much infra-red equipment you might have, and however many hours you may sit up waiting in your photographer's hide, you'll never catch a concept with a camera. But radio, in creating its own verbal world, finds a natural

9

territory in abstraction and the imagination, and ideas come running like little creatures to St Francis. The only criterion is how well a speaker performs the task which radio demands: to discourse rather than to describe.

The programmes on which this book is based are therefore not so much about architecture as about the way architecture is thought about. Nor are they in any sense objective or comprehensive. On the contrary, they are very specifically about what was in the architectural air in the early 1980s, and what a number of lively, opinionated people had on their minds. Again like ripples on a pond, the programmes do assume either a certain knowledge of what caused the ripples to be made in the first place, or that in listening to – or reading – what is said, some sense of the stone that caused those ripples will be implied.

The programmes were made and broadcast on Radio 3 between 1981 and 1984. In *Behind the Façade*, they have been threaded together in an order that enables one chapter to throw light upon another. *What Revival?* takes the temperature of architectural ideas that were beginning to crystallise at the turn of the decade. *Digging Graves* is an interview with an American architect in whom many of those ideas are embodied. *A Magnificent Catastrophe* contrasts American theory with American practice, taking New York as its example of the real pressures which shape the making of cities. *The Best Hated Architect in the World* is an interview with an architect who, no less than his buildings, has become the very mascot of New York. *Sir Edwin Lutyens: The Empire Strikes Back* and *The Reversible Mackintosh* consider the rise of two turn-of-the-century British architects to new-found popularity. *Walter Gropius's Crystal Visions* looks, conversely, at how the same tide of fortune has diminished the standing of one of this century's most important pioneers. And, finally, *Sounds Unsound* tests the idea of functionalism – which Gropius did so much to promote – in the design of concert halls.

What Revival?

Every year, the Queen bestows a Gold Medal on a distinguished contributor to architecture. This invariably goes to a British architect, but writers and architects from abroad have also been honoured, especially since the war. In 1982, the medal was awarded to Berthold Lubetkin, the pioneering Russian architect who came to England in 1931 after working briefly in Paris.

The award was long overdue. Lubetkin's best work had been carried out within ten years of his arrival here, most notably under Julian, later Sir Julian, Huxley and Solly, now Lord, Zuckerman at Regent's Park Zoo, where he created one of modern architecture's most enduring icons – the Penguin Pool, with its interlocking spiral ramps. His career, however, was short-lived. In 1949, he was appointed Chief Architect for Peterlee New Town, but the job was dogged with disagreement and after two years he resigned – not just from Peterlee but from architecture altogether – to become, extraordinarily, a pig farmer. He was not seen in architectural circles again until the award ceremony for his medal.

To many architects, Lubetkin's resignation felt like a betrayal, though the failure of the progressive architectural establishment to support him and recognise his achievements at the time can be taken the same way. Which is why it came as a surprise that the Royal Institute of British Architects should have advised the Queen that Lubetkin was the man to honour in 1982. Why then? Why not before?

To some extent, Lubetkin was the innocent beneficiary of a change in architectural tastes. Disillusion with modern architecture had got to such a pitch by the 1970s that architects and writers were increasingly looking back to the 1920s and 30s, back to the early days of modern architecture, to try and rediscover what its original intentions were, what its strengths and weaknesses were, what had gone wrong, and how else it might have developed. Different people found different things. In America, a number of academically-minded architects, working independently but known as the New York Five or The Whites, proposed through their designs and their writings that the white-box Cubist architecture of Le Corbusier had expired before its time, and that it contained ideas that deserved taking further. (One of these five was Michael Graves, who talks about his work in Chapter 2, and whose own tastes turned rapidly from the intellectual purity of early Cubism to the more debased, more popular forms of Modernism that emerged from its contact with fashion and the market place.) Interior designers were also struck by the 1930s styles, from the exoticism of grand hotels and ocean liners to the jazz effects of Art Deco and tacky neon lighting. It was as if everyone suddenly wanted to be a character from *Brideshead Revisited*, *The Great Gatsby* or Dashiell Hammett.

Designers found source material waiting to be rediscovered. So did historians and conservationists, and one of the more curious offshoots was the formation in 1979 of an English group called the Thirties Society that dedicated itself to the protection of the most characteristic buildings of the 1920s and 30s. In some ways, the society seemed more like a social romp for Noël Coward manqués. There was no doubting, however, the commitment and expertise of its founding members, or of its patrons, among them Sir John Betjeman, Roy Strong, and Norman St John Stevas. As a pressure group, it was less effective in preventing the destruction of 1930s buildings than in lamenting their passing once they were gone, but it did put on very good parties.

The Thirties Society was a symptom of changing attitudes. People were wanting to have fun, and wanting architecture to be fun after years of intellectualised austerity. Perhaps the Bauhaus and CIAM (Congrès Internationaux d'Architecture Moderne) had not been as earnest as we now remember them. Odd photographs and surviving descriptions suggested that they could also be regarded – in their early days, at least – as high-spirited social meeting grounds where participants were far more exuberant, wayward, and promiscuous – intellectually and in other ways – than they wished to appear. Perhaps their own reports of their activities had made them out to be more concordant and purposeful than they really were. Perhaps writers who only knew of them at a distance had promoted their cause too puritanically instead of homing in on individual motivations and struggles for power.[1] That was the new line.

In the 1980s, it was precisely the promise of new revelations about old personalities which rekindled interest in them, and made it possible for the first time to engage with them as ordinary clay-footed mortals. Suddenly, architects like Lubetkin were in demand again from journalists and historians who, whatever they thought of them as architectural leaders, recognised what funds of amusing stories they must possess.

At its most harmless, it was gossip-column stuff but there was also a more sinister side to it. The pioneer architects prided themselves on having eliminated questions of decoration and style from architecture, and reduced – or elevated – it to its essentials: materials, function, and abstract composition. The new interpretation of this compared such elimination to the acting out of racial purity laws. Architecture, it was said, had been stripped of its variety – a harmless ploy as long as it remained the in-joke of a small architectural clique, but devastating when taken up and ruthlessly applied as the orthodoxy of a new world order – International Modernism.

The analogy was enticingly simple, and capable of colouring the most innocent of events. The week before the presentation of Lubetkin's award, the Architectural Association in London put on a pre-emptive evening of 1930s nostalgia. The AA is both a club for architects and lay devotees, and a college with an independent and avant-garde history. On this particular evening in June 1982, seventy of its members turned up to the 'Revolution Dinner' as it was called to hear the reminiscences of veterans from the

---

[1]Nikolaus Pevsner, who wrote enthusiastically about the Bauhaus during and after its ascendancy, and was later made an honorary member of the Bauhaus Archiv in West Berlin, did not visit Dessau, the home of the Bauhaus, until 1978.

heroic past, among them the engineer Sir Ove Arup, the historian Sir John Summerson, the writer Sir James Richards, Walter Gropius's English partner Maxwell Fry, and Jack Pritchard who had helped to bring Gropius to England. (Both men talk about Gropius in Chapter 7.)

It was a curious gathering at which a spirit of unfulfilled idealism could be detected in the air. In other circumstances – in Bolivia or Paraguay, perhaps – it could equally have been a clandestine *Stammtisch* of ex-Nazis. In the eyes of the conservation groups, these were the men who had inspired the destruction of Europe's historic towns and cities. Conrad Jameson had already labelled them as 'war criminals' in 1979, though had he said so that evening, he would probably have had to contend with an unceremonious expulsion at the hands of a pair of hefty Corbusian bouncers. If anyone had thought it was going to be an evening of apology, they had miscalculated. The message seemed to be that if anyone was guilty, it was *us* for having failed *them*, not the other way round.

The idea that these men had in their time represented an architectural conspiracy, however, had all the hallmarks of a conspiracy itself. It was nevertheless cheekily maintained by a handful of right-wing polemicists and academics who themselves had ambitions to capture the intellectual initiative from the left, infiltrate the Conservative party in the guise of policy advisers and strategists, and thereby shift the political mood of the country to the right. Their centres were London and Cambridge, their organs the *Spectator* and the *Salisbury Review*, with *Country Life* as their architectural rallying point. Figures such as David Watkin asserted that pre-war propagandists for modern architecture had shared the same rhetorical style as Nazis and Marxists, and that they were therefore guided by the same inhuman contempt for the individual.

'Individuality' was the key word here, for it was the individual who was held up as the main victim of the tyranny of modern architecture. In his name, a new tyranny would be enacted: a nationwide return to a perceived tradition of building – with Georgian architecture at its apex – in which, to state it crudely, any architecture rooted in the nineteenth century or earlier was legitimate, while that rooted in the twentieth century was not.

That was one aspect of the architecture scene in the early 1980s. Another was going on within architecture, where a struggle was taking place that echoed the nineteenth-century Battle of the Styles. That had been a fight for supremacy between

Gothic architecture (representing Romanticism and national virtues) and classicism (representing a larger, more enlightened internationalism.) One hundred years on, the battle was between the new Gothic architecture of *all* the styles and the new classicism of none. Gothic was winning.

'Style', like 'individuality', was another key word, and one which had been causing difficulties for some time. To Le Corbusier, *le style* was a classic quality – a distillation of form, achieved by everyday objects only after years, even centuries, of use and modification. It was a quality which he, Picasso, Léger and Ozenfant had given attention to in their semi-abstract paintings of wine bottles and guitars. But this was not the only meaning of the word. 'Style' could be used in the looser sense of 'panache' or 'elegance' – qualities verging dangerously on the borderline of art and fashion, and capable of being applied to the architect himself as well as to his work. Lubetkin could be called a stylish architect; even more so, the Hungarian architect Ernö Goldfinger, who had also made his home in England.

More problematic was a third definition of 'style' as a characteristic manner of expression. To say in the 1930s that a modern building was in the style of its architect was ideologically unsound; to say that it conformed to the Modern *style*, like a church in the Romanesque style or a palace in the Baronial style, or that it was 'modernistic', was outright heresy, because it was felt that architecture had finally arrived at its ultimate destination, dispensing with stylistic problems once and for all. This utopian claim is what the new generation found least convincing, since changes in architectural styles between 1930 and 1980 showed only too clearly that pre-war architecture had been as typical of its time as Ovaltine, Jarrow and the Duchess of Windsor.

The impact of this apparently tiny observation was enormous; if the pioneers were guilty of a crime that they themselves had invented, the whole problem of style became self-cancelling, which in turn lifted the taboo on imagery and decoration. It was like opening Pandora's box. Upstairs from the Revolution Dinner at the AA, an end-of-year exhibition of student work showed how wild the contents of that box could be. The walls were alive with drawings of classical pediments, Doric columns, industrial gantries, Cubist façades, oculus windows, Charles Rennie Mackintosh trellis-work, Hollywood sunbursts, Rock-and-Roll starbursts, oversized keystones, marble claddings, skewed grids and symmetry – all characteristically executed in pale-pastel cross-hatching, smudge-shadowed with Venus colouring pencils.

If the Revolution Dinner resembled an expatriate German drinking club, the exhibition above was more like a revivalist prayer meeting. Everyone seemed to be, if not foaming at the mouth, then at least speaking in tongues. Ten years earlier, the initials 'AA' might just as well have stood for Anti-Architecture; the school was all participatory politics, pop sociology, squats, communes, geodesic domes, instant cities, inflatables, tensiles, bubbles, pods, demountables, garbage housing and science fiction. Now a new generation had sprung up speaking pidgin forms of languages they had no prior knowledge of – languages which were often historically in opposition to each other – and speaking them simultaneously. Like revivalists, their outpourings, while untutored and barely understood, seemed innate and irrepressible.

In the light of these events the RIBA nominated Berthold Lubetkin for the Gold Medal. It was a symbolic gesture designed to rescue him from the Young Fogeys, to mark his achievements of fifty years earlier, and to reinforce their own embattled professional dogmas by getting a long-overlooked prophet to pronounce his benediction over them.

Mr Lubetkin was glad to oblige, and used the presentation ceremony to denounce the events that had inadvertently restored him to prominence. 'After not having read an architectural book for twenty years,' he said in an interview at the time,[1] 'I suddenly realised that everything I valued was in deadly danger. I could have written an article about it but no one would have taken any notice. Receiving the medal gives me the opportunity to shout it from the roof top of the Pantheon, so to speak. If there's anything I have to say to the profession, it's Wake up and Stop Fiddling. We're not living in a period when we can play around anymore. We're facing the decay of civilisation and these [people] are knifing us in the back.'

The passion of Lubetkin's outcry gives some flavour of how seriously the issues were being taken, and how entrenched were the opposing camps. But just how different were their respective positions? Lubetkin's concern seemed to be that modern architecture had been hijacked by history, and yet history was not really the main threat. During the design of his two blocks of flats on Highgate Hill – Highpoint One and Highpoint Two – he had worked with Palladio's *Quattro Libri* at his elbow, ever aware that he was re-enacting time-honoured rules of harmonic proportion

---

[1] Interview with Stephen Games in the *London Standard*, 29 June 1982.

in his designs. Nor was he worried by the academicism of the new historians. His own interest in architecture had itself been incidental to his interest in Western philosophy; architecture was simply the vehicle through which that interest had expressed itself, which is why he found it relatively easy to give up in 1951.

What really offended Lubetkin was the irrationality of architecture in the 1980s, which he saw as a sign both of ignorance and wilfulness. He believed that history, whether addressed in the name of novelty or continuity, was diverting the architect from his job of making rational choices – of using architecture as a vehicle for order, logic, and lucid clarity in a world that was otherwise chaotic. 'The sleep of Reason begets monsters,' he said in his Gold Medal address, quoting from a painting by Goya, 'and here are those monsters in architecture too. Buildings with all their devastating wit, synthetic whimsicality and startling novelty promoted by the fashion trade. This is transvestite architecture – Hepplewhite and Chippendale in drag.' He also reminded his audience of how Hitler, echoing Nietzsche, had instructed his artists to rely on instinct. 'Let us remember this when we hear the drumbeat to return to vernacular tradition. . . . There is no future mechanically contained in the past. The process of renewal implies change, not merely accumulation.'

Such was the climate in 1982, with rhetoric flying on all sides, and calls to arms, and sworn enemies accusing one another of being the real fascist ('You're a Nazi.' 'No *you're* a Nazi.'). And it was the climate in which the documentaries and interviews on which this book is based were made. The first programme *What Revival?* was designed to test the claims and counter-claims that were then current by talking to five architects or architectural writers who had either taught at the Architectural Association, or whose views seemed to be of some influence there. Was historical revivalism, whether freakish and fragmented or conservative and conventional, really as much of a *volte-face* as it might appear to be?

The reintroduction of historic imagery does not constitute a rejection of intellectual theory. On the contrary, imagery is often made a way of continuing theoretical debates that are already taking place. But it does introduce a new dilemma. Where modern design once tried to hold back for as long as was possible before finally committing itself to a finished form, architecture is now suffering from the difficulty of premature ejaculation. Overall appearance has become much more the starting point in the design process, replacing the Modernist maxim 'Form follows Function' with the more up-to-date 'Function follows Form'. With some students, the cry goes up: 'I just like it that way' when asked to explain themselves; with architects, the need to rationalise is not so easily abandoned, which has led more thoughtful members of the profession into some tricky soul-searching as they have struggled to renegotiate their positions.

One such architect is Jeremy Dixon who studied at the Architectural Association in the 1960s and now teaches there. He has recently won commissions to design the extension to the Royal Opera House, Covent Garden, together with Bill Jack of BDP, and to refurbish the restaurant at the Tate Gallery. This follows on from his modernisation of the same gallery's coffee shop, which he based on the 1812 Breakfast Room that Sir John Soane designed for his house in Lincoln's Inn Fields – as if there were something about Soane's shallow-domed dish-like ceilings which suggested light meals. In another recent work – a publicly-funded speculative housing development in Maida Vale – he developed a prototype house based loosely on early nineteenth-century villas in the nearby area, an approach he had previously adopted in North Kensington. There, a corner development took its aesthetic cues from the surrounding Victorian brick terraces, but synthesised in the style of Mondrian. It was all a very long way from the first project he designed – an estate of terraced housing in Milton Keynes, very much like a length of extruded aluminium in appearance, with protruding flanges separating each housing unit from the next.

'Fifteen years ago,' says Dixon, 'one's intellectual horizon was very much defined by a system of thought broadly called the Modern Movement. On the other hand one was going round London constantly horrified by what was happening. The curious thing is that a lot of that destruction was not done in the name of commercial gain but in the name of what could be broadly called a social programme, and done by people with the best motives – by the most intelligent members of their profession. One explanation for that is that housing had become a monument to a social programme and a muddle had arisen about the expression of the exceptional building and the ordinary building.

'If one looks at the history of London, it's a city that's been unfortified since William the Conqueror, and it's spread out as a loose suburban pattern. In fact there was a decree in the time of Elizabeth I banning the building of flats. Paris, by contrast, is a series of concentric rings or fortified walls. This has led to a gradual concentration of the city, a very early acceptance of the flat as a way of living and, as a result, a particular balance between private dwellings and public spaces. In this way, public spaces have become essential adjuncts to the flat because it's a rather second-rate dwelling, or at least, not ideal. And one gets a very different balance between the private space and the public space in the two cities.'

What Paris and London share, however, is an overall hierarchy. 'The classical notion of the city consists of a background texture of ordinary stuff, and then exceptional pieces like churches which act as monuments. This changed in the twentieth century. All buildings became in some way exceptional. The Modern Movement tended to see architecture as setting up a problem and solving it, and that became associated with the "unique solution". So you got almost all the objects in the city being built as objects internal to themselves – unique solutions solving a particular thing.

'I don't mind the Modern Movement at all when it deals with big buildings. In a curious way it's extremely appropriate to monuments. It's the ordinary which is the problem, the imbalance in the city between texture and monument. And it's that that projects me in a search for some kind of historical position. If one takes the starting point as the texture of the city, you're not so much making individual buildings as making the spaces which lie between them. And so one's actually looking at what the language of street making might be. The first move I made when I did my North Kensington housing scheme was to see housing as having an element of continuity – an element of the known and the expected, as opposed to the quality of the monument, which is concerned with surprise and exception and of special solution.'

Jeremy Dixon's position owes much to the American architect and writer Robert Venturi whose first seminal book, *Complexity and Contradiction in Architecture*, appeared in 1966. In it, Venturi spoke out on behalf of the man in the street, arguing that people wanted a richness of experience which strict modern architecture was failing to supply. What he meant was a richness of visual experience, illustrated in his book through photographs of, for example, medieval European cities in which twisting alleyways provided constantly changing vistas, and arched openings modulated the rhythm of light and shade. In a later book, *Learning from Las Vegas*, published in 1972, Venturi showed how this richness of experience could operate in the modern world, and specifically in the apparent cultural desert of American suburbia. His message was that architects needed to rediscover the commonplace, and he commended the naïvety with which non-architects expressed themselves architecturally. His model was Main Street USA, where the built environment depends for its survival on how clearly, and how loudly, it communicates its various identities. He pointed to neon signs, to hot-dog stalls shaped like hot-dogs, and to mail-order catalogue accessories which convert a house into a Home Beautiful.

It was a very American, and very commercial, message though its language was that of Roland Barthes and French sociolinguistics, which in turn depended on Marxist literary theory. Barthes had been interested less in the ostensible meaning of a text than in the hidden and unintentional meanings locked up in the words it used. By defining these, he showed how language could communicate a range of values, prejudices and preconceptions quite independent of what the writer had intended to say. This was known as the sub-text, and words being examined for their sub-textual meanings were called *signs*. Hence, this form of analysis was called *semiology*, the study of sign language, or *semiotics* – previously a medical term for the study of symptoms.

Barthes then borrowed the semiological techniques he was already using in the study of language in order to study popular culture. Between 1954 and 1956, he wrote a number of essays under the title *Mythologies* – for which he is perhaps best known in Britain – in which he treated human behaviour as if it were a literary text containing unintentional cultural messages. It was a fruitful exercise and he used it to argue that this method of analysis proved that bourgeois culture was degenerate. Since the bourgeois were greedy and acquisitive, he said, they communicated too many messages at once, and messages which were complex, confused, and contradictory. Contradiction and complexity were not, however, of any consequence to the bourgeois since they were only interested in the quantity and consumption rather than quality of experience.

What Robert Venturi did was to turn Barthes' technique against him. Since Barthes' argument stemmed from his prior belief in the degeneracy of the bourgeoisie, Venturi – who, as an American bourgeois, was implicitly attacked – defended himself and his culture by turning the attack on bourgeois culture into a defence of it. Complexity and contradiction therefore became expressions of approval – they pointed to abundance of experience, to cultural freedom, to the validity of personal expression no matter how debased, and to the absence of dogma.

Venturi made it possible to read American suburbia as a

powerhouse of cultural messages. The cross-referencing of architectural features within the same building – Colonial ranch-style balloon-frame bungalows with Tudor leaded windows, Spanish hacienda tiles, sub-Bernini porches on vine-clad Doric columns, and external random-rubble Mexican chimneys – became a dictionary of middle-class aspirations. Buildings which contained a plethora of stylistic references were regarded as rich, eloquent, human, witty, ironic and ambiguous. It became immediately apparent that when judged by these standards, modern architecture in the International Style failed because it failed to communicate, or communicated only the anonymous messages that one associated with, for example, international corporations.

Robert Venturi is the intellectual father-figure of the movement to which Jeremy Dixon belongs, and he appreciates the intentions of the generation which he has inspired. 'I think all architects, all artists, must rely on the past whether they want to or not. They are in a context that involves the past.

'In my younger days when I was more literally a modern archi-tect, in the period when modern architecture officially disdained history and the reliance on history for forms and symbolism, we went to history for general lessons concerning space and form and texture and rhythm – for all the abstract elements of architecture. But at that time, we did not go to history for the symbolism – for the iconography that's involved in history. Now, in this later period, I think many of us are including that dimension as well, and learning from history about symbolism and ornament.

'I think, you know, there are several approaches to art. There's some art that's very good just for its clarity. An early Renaissance chapel is strong for that reason, because it is simple; for modern architecture, that was the ideal. But there's another kind of art – let's say, an early Christian or Byzantine chapel, where you go in and you say "Oh wow! It's wonderful!" – not because it's clear and unified but because it's rich and has many dimensions. I think we're related more to the latter kind of art. We're in a period when we're needing layerings of messages and rich effects.'

The positions occupied by Robert Venturi and Jeremy Dixon are by no means the only example of new architectural policies being formulated on the basis of a re-reading of the traditional city. Peter Hodgkinson also trained at the Architectural Association in the early 1960s. In 1966 he left England and went to Barcelona to work for the Catalan architect Ricardo Bofill. Bofill had a reputa-tion as a flamboyant playboy with a background in anti-Fascist activism. His great passion, he was once quoted as saying, was to make love in cemeteries, and he let it be known that he wanted, through his buildings, to receive the kind of adulation usually reserved for pop stars. His earliest work in Spain was inspired by Catalan mythology and science fiction. He topped a hillside monument on the French–Spanish border with four twisted red-brick columns, intended to symbolise King Wilfred the Hairy, first king of the Catalans, who scratched four fingermarks of blood across his chest as an oath to keep out the Moors. He also designed a housing estate called 'Walden 7' after Thoreau's *Walden* and B. F. Skinner's *Waldens two to six* – novels about communities conditioned to be happy. A more recent development on the outskirts of Paris is called 'Xanadu'. As a publicist, Bofill's ways could not be regarded as subtle.

After nearly twenty years with Bofill's practice, the *Taller de Arquitectura*, Peter Hodgkinson is now one of the two project directors in charge of Bofill's operations in Paris. Among these is a housing scheme at Marne-la-Vallée called the Palace of Abraxas which you might well mistake for a Roman amphitheatre if you flew over it in a hurry. Like all the work of the *Taller*, it represents not so much the informed disillusion that Jeremy Dixon felt about the Modern Movement as an ebullient disdain for the rest of the architectural profession. Housing estates that look like housing estates reduce people to drones; so give them Versailles and raise them to princes.

'Mass housing is usually produced by architects of low aesthetic abilities,' says Peter Hodgkinson. 'Many are not even architects; they're just building technicians. They've probably never heard of Palladio or Brunelleschi or Le Corbusier. But they've been conditioned to design in a vulgarised version of what one could call the International Style. This is the worst possible model because it was based on one-off buildings by the great masters – Le Corbusier, Alvar Aalto, Frank Lloyd Wright – buildings that were special and unique and should never have been copied.'

This does not mean that Peter Hodgkinson disapproves of copying, as long as it copies the right models. 'If the classical tradition had persisted, many of the cities which have completely lost their identity would still have that identity, and many of our villages and towns would not have been destroyed.

'Take Bath. Bath was built all in one go by a small group of financiers and developers and architects who could *impose* – and this is the important word – *impose* their will on the general public. It was planned in a grand urban manner with crescents and squares that were then divided up into smaller lots and sold off to private developers. But they were sold with the façade drawn on the site plan, which joined up with the next façade on either side. So that although you had thirty-five developers in one street, they all more or less followed the same line. This was the ideal situation. And it works – in Bath, in Edinburgh New Town, in Brighton. They are all towns which grew up very quickly, like housing estates. So within the *Taller Bofill*, we look to Bath as a dream model – by no means utopian, but totally realistic. And I think that more and more architects and planners will start looking at Georgian or Regency planning, and the equivalent in France, for lessons as to how to deal with the future. Because unless you apply such rules, you're not going to be able to build properly.'

But how can the Bath model adapt itself to the infrastructure of the modern city? 'Infrastructure was far more complicated in Georgian times than it is today,' says Hodgkinson. 'The horse and cart made far more noise, and far more mess, and were far less efficient than their modern equivalent. What we're talking about goes beyond whether Roman chariots are racing from the Circus Maximus to the Senate House. I don't think the Senate would have been designed any differently if the Jaguar XK120 existed. I think as an architectural model Bath is totally applicable today, and even if within fifty years we all have mini-helicopters or rockets and the entire world is heated with solar energy, the model will be equally as valuable.'

The Cambridge art historian David Watkin agrees. 'The classical language of architecture has been the mainstay of European architecture from the earliest times up to the twentieth century,' he says, 'and it would be unlikely if that tradition were to be permanently interrupted. After all, it does have very great relevance. After having attempted to dismiss it for thirty or forty years, one can perhaps see that those years were untypical in the history of architecture, and we're now returning to what has been the norm for the several centuries before that.

'In architecture, classicism is a kind of grammar, and this can be treated in very different ways in different countries, at different times, and by different architects. Architecture does change – this is the marvel of it – so that we can date it fairly precisely on largely stylistic grounds and different phases of the classical tradition.'

Does that mean that classical architecture can be applied to buildings of the present day? 'I think that you could have asked the same question in the fifteenth and sixteenth centuries when architects were reviving the forms of Roman architecture and adapting them to purposes which hadn't been seen before. Modern architects are faced with the same challenge. When the Essex architect Quinlan Terry was designing a large Bahai temple in Persia a few years ago, he found that the classical articulation of the interior was a tremendous help to him in laying things like ventilation ducts and air conditioning units and lighting plugs and boxes, and that they fitted beautifully into these classical pilasters and mouldings, whereas in a modern building they would give tremendous visual trouble.'

But a Bahai temple is a rare example of a building where extravagance and conservatism might be regarded as appropriate. The question is, how would Dr Watkin propose that a classical architect design a power station or a multi-storey car park? 'I don't know why you press on those particular buildings,' he replies, 'which are clearly going to be adapted with very great difficulty to the classical tradition, when there are so many other types of buildings like housing which can and are being adapted.' One cannot take a consistent view for all architecture in society. 'I think pluralism is probably the position that we're coming to, where different styles are seen as suitable for different building types.'

Dr Watkin's pluralism is not, however, one which admits freedom of choice. On the contrary, it demarcates specific styles to specific functions quite inflexibly. It is not, then, a genuine pluralism nor is pluralism its ambition. 'I don't value anything that has been developed in the Modern Movement, but clearly so many people do that it is not going to be thrown over overnight, and will continue to be used for a wide variety of functions. My belief is that classicism could be used probably for those large and complex purposes such as power stations or airports providing you had an architect of large imagination like Lutyens or Wren or Brunelleschi. But at the moment we haven't.'

A more generous example of stylistic demarcation can be seen in the newly-built Clore Wing of the Tate Gallery. Designed by James Stirling, Michael Wilford and Associates, the idea of the building is an appealing one: that the exterior should respond, chameleon-like, in different ways to different parts of the site. This means grandeur alongside the main steps and portico of the old building, neutrality down the long side wall, and utilitarianism at the back, where the service entrance is. Stirling interprets utilitarianism as something akin to 1930s Modernism – the factory aesthetic – treating it in his own characteristic way, as he has done before, with brightly-coloured metal handrails, strip windows, and a ship's funnel. Here there is a good reason for assigning the modernistic façade to the service quarters; the context requires it. But the idea of context gets so out of hand elsewhere in the building that it begins to suffer from stylistic indigestion. The main façade is faced in coloured stucco panels which modulate from the red of the Queen Anne house which stands at the front corner of the site, through orange, to the yellowy-grey stone of the Tate Gallery itself. In between, there are allusions to Minoan tombs, portcullises, Elizabethan parapets, Mackintosh oriels, and – like Jeremy Dixon's coffee shop – Sir John Soane. But why? Is this Lubetkin's monster begot by the sleep of Reason?

It has never quite been established how it was that James Stirling went from being a leading explorer of the new to a leading pasticheur of the old. One man who has taken the credit for his conversion is Leon Krier, one of two Luxembourgeois brothers who have gone on to become influential polemicists on architecture and urban theory. Rob Krier teaches in Belgium and has recently designed a courtyard housing scheme on the Ritterstrasse in West Berlin as a twenty-three-piece jigsaw to be completed by his own and six other architectural practices. In its conception, its planning and its execution, the scheme was intended as a didactic political gesture.

Younger brother Leon lives in London, where he teaches occasionally at the Architectural Association. From 1968–70, and again between 1973–74, he worked in Stirling's office and it is suggested that he made his influence felt – though this is not a suggestion that Stirling has acknowledged. So far, Leon Krier has not built anything of his own, but he enters competitions and works on imaginary schemes for replanning the world's major cities in an other-worldly, de Chiricesque style. Like David Watkin in his book *Morality and Architecture*, he points to the sins carried out in the name of progress and argues that the question of whether classical architecture is appropriate in the modern world is a red herring. It is not the appropriateness of classical architecture which is in doubt but that of contemporary society, he says.

'One says that society has moved on in order to justify unpopular changes. People are put into barrack-like housing in new towns and post-war housing estates on the grounds that one can't do anything else. But it isn't true. It is a matter of the skill of the architect.

'Urban highways, multi-storey car parks, nuclear power stations – all these buildings are part of the disarray we live in.

Society has been so demolished in its cohesion that virtually every action you do is interfered with by a machine. I have to run a car which was built in France on petrol which comes from Saudi Arabia. All this is totally unnecessary. Just see what architecture is the most comfortable today: it's not the American cities with their highways or the new towns which are just big roundabouts and wasted land, but the old cities. These are the cities which have adapted the best to the car. Any business company in London that can afford it is located in the City or the West End. They don't go to new towns – not just for reasons of prestige but also for comfort; old towns are more human.'

Leon Krier's attack on industrialised society recalls William Morris's *News from Nowhere* of 1888. Here, Morris also posed solutions, pointing to a direct correspondence between medieval thatched cottages and a contented, fair-faced, socially-minded, uncompetitive population, and visualising a London of the future that had both. It was an argument which believed deeply that integrity could be judged on appearances. This is why it showed such faith in architectural style.

Leon Krier's own designs show a similar correspondence between an idealised architecture and an idealised population. His drawings are inhabited by a pedestrianised proletariat for ever bowing stiffly to each other as they take the air, *en famille*, on Sunday afternoon strolls around a town whose skyline and regular street pattern is only allowed to be interrupted – and then in a deliberately mannered way – by churches and public buildings. Residential buildings are uniformly the six and seven-storey apartment houses found on the Continent, but in Krier's case featuring elements of the most primitive construction – symbolic rooftop temples and over-scaled wooden gantries used, perhaps, for hauling furniture to the upper floors but more significant as ornaments or icons of a pre-Modern age. It is an urban image which promises much for civic order but little for individual non-conformity. Ritual and continuity are everything.

'What I'm interested in,' says Krier, 'is classicism as a principle, and I would define classical architecture as everything which was done, let's say, before industrialisation – from Gothic right back to the Athens of the fourth century before Christ. The forms may be very different but the philosophical principles of that architecture are very much the same.'

In order to make his case for continuity, Leon Krier has had to embrace the most extreme interpretations of classicism. For several years, for example, he has been collecting material on

Hitler's architect Albert Speer, the man who built the Zeppelin-feld for the Nuremberg rallies and planned a New Berlin of vast proportions – a city which, like the Reich, would last for a thousand years and finally achieve immortality in the glory of its ruins. Krier recognises that his polemical need to take in Speer can be embarrassing.

'I would very much have preferred it if Hitler had adored Henry Moore and maybe taken Le Corbusier instead of Albert Speer as his chief architect. After all, if you look at a Henry Moore sculpture, it's far more inhuman than even the most inhuman Fascist sculpture because it is very difficult to recognise it as even the work of a human being. As for building, people say that classical architecture or rows of columns are the expression of totalitarianism or repression. It isn't true. I think I could even imagine living in the Chancellery of Albert Speer you know, I wouldn't mind that. I think most people would find it quite elegant, if one took away the swastikas and the flags. Classicism really transcends the limits of any political period or tenancy. And that is why you can revive it – because it is completely independent of political expression.'

But classical architecture is made up of a hierarchy of elements in a fixed relationship to each other, which can be used to imply a fixed social order and a denial of liberty. It also lends itself to theatrical effects and monumental gestures which can be put to the use of the state. Leon Krier disagrees.

'Monumentality happened to be the taste of one particular tyranny. You have to see Nazism not so much as the invention of 1930 but as the culmination of a certain tendency which was in industrial culture from the start. It is really the modernity of somebody like Speer or of his type of architecture which frightens me. This kind of industrial repetitiveness, the emphasis on size, on breaking yet another limit. Look at any tyranny nowadays. They couldn't care less about neo-classicism or any other style. They are just happy with their television and that sort of software. Electronic stuff – that's much more totalitarian than any columns.'

Inspired perhaps by Speer's monumentality, Ricardo Bofill's Theatre of the Palace of Abraxas at Marne-la-Vallée wears classical clothing but rises a grotesquely unclassical ten storeys. Normally, the use of classical ornament prevents buildings from rising more than four or five storeys. Confronted with this prob-lem on early skyscrapers, American architects trained in the Beaux-Arts tradition broke the building down into three parts – a base, a shaft, and a pediment. As long as the base and pediment retained some sense of scale, the shaft in between could be of indefinite height. Bofill's work uses a similar strategy, breaking the façade into three bands. But at the Theatre, the bands are all of *equal* height instead of being separated by a central band of *greater* height, so that the building appears simultaneously overpowering and squat. In addition, each band contains three floors of windows alternating with paired three-storey Tuscan columns. The columns are relatively small – much smaller than if Bofill had run them up the whole ten storeys. But Bofill runs *other* columns up the ten-storey height – grossly-oversized single fluted columns containing the staircases. Once again, there is a sensation of squatness and giantism. Another monster begot while Reason sleeps?

'Bofill's classicism is what I'd call "reinterpreted classicism",' says Peter Hodgkinson. 'It's about understanding the language of classicism and the technology it's using. This is very clear if you go and look at Marne-la-Vallée. You'll see the building is a complete expression of heavy concrete panel technology, which is normally extremely unpleasant and cold. But we've converted it into a new language with the introduction of colour and richness and different mouldings. That gives you another vocabulary, and not simply a classical copy of a Georgian terrace house.'

Marne-la-Vallée takes an ornamental language developed for the mason's chisel and applies it to the concrete mould. Given the money, would Hodgkinson's team rather be building in stone? 'Not now,' he says, 'because we think we're on our way to a breakthrough in concrete where we can make it not just look like stone but become in a way superior to stone. Some of the new samples covered in various oxidising chemicals with fixatives look like beautifully soft marble. I mean, they actually glow. And thus we can start having houses which are factory-built and assembled on site. But when they're finished they don't look like our image of a concrete house, but like a homage to Palladio.

'We're also trying to make the plans as classical as we can. One Italian architect has built a miniature Palladian Villa Rotunda in which the hall in the middle is the dining room, and the kitchen is the big room on the right and so on. We're not trying to do that. We're trying to find out the essence of the composition, of the proportion and the liveability of the spaces which Palladio created, and reduce these to modern sizes, and then build them with materials which are in themselves of noble aspect, and then sell them at a low market price.'

In the end, however, Marne-la-Vallée is everything that it wants not to be – a vast, mechanical, repetitive composition, desperately anxious about admitting its own identity. Where it strives for grandeur, it acts out instead an empty charade that is both disappointing and intimidating. This does not mean that the motives of the *Taller Bofill* were dishonest. But it may mean that ornament is less adaptable than they would like to think, and that significant but unintended changes of meaning take place when an architectural style is wrenched out of its normal context and used in a different way.

'A style is a product of its time,' says Jeremy Dixon, 'and that includes the balance between the different craft skills and the available technology. And I think it's very difficult to impose a decorative system from one architectural mode onto a building built now, unless you learn the whole grammar and actually build it in the same way.'

Jeremy Dixon's solution has been to distance his ornamentation from its nineteenth-century sources, interpreting it more abstractly than literally. Having observed carved stone copings on the tops of brick gate-posts in the streets of North Kensington, he has replied with plain concrete pyramids. Victorian bay windows are suggested by protruding wood-and-glass cages. Ornamental fretwork around the gables and the doorways is echoed in square ornamental trellis-work. Traditional relationships are also matched – half-flights of steps leading from the pavement up to front doors, half-flights down to basements, left-right reversals of plan which result in pairs of front doors alternating with pairs of windows, and street façades more formal than the backs.

Jeremy Dixon can work in this way because he has not entirely abandoned the values he grew up with. He still values abstract relationships more highly than visual gestures, which gives him the freedom to reinterpret visual forms in the way he does. However, abstraction and ornamentation operate by different rules, and however hard a modern architect might try to bring ornamentation to heel by reordering it intellectually, ornament can remain as stubborn and uncooperative as an old dog. The visual world is more immediate than the cerebral, so that when one reinterprets a familiar form, one is first struck not by its familiarity but by its distortion. How confident is Jeremy Dixon that the man in the street will recognise the relationships he had intended him to see, rather than be offended by their freakishness?

'You can't be certain,' he replies. 'In that scheme in North Kensington, I was interested in experimenting with elements that might be historical, or something to do with the locality, or Modern Movement, so that you bring together a mixture which has not perhaps been seen before. Whether it's all that recognisable to the passer-by, I don't think matters, actually. It's giving *oneself* a way of operating that allows things gradually to be embellished and made richer.'

Similar moves are taking place all over Europe and America, but not in a way that pleases Robert Venturi. 'In general, I'm kind of horrified at a lot of what's going on,' he says, 'especially if some of it is the result of things I've said. Someone has said: "God save me from my friends, I can take care of my enemies," and I think some of the older architects are beginning to say the same thing about their followers. The main problem is that people don't understand very well what you're saying. For instance, when we wrote the book *Learning from Las Vegas*, people had the idea that the main message might have been entitled "Liking Las Vegas". The whole thing got very mixed up. The main subject of the book was actually symbolism in architecture, as a way to get at a new iconography and be more tolerant of different taste cultures. That was not understood.

'There is also the fact that people take you up and then exaggerate your position. It is very easy to be an extremist. The way to get attention in the press is to make extreme statements. But usually, art is complex and the message is complex and it isn't all a matter of coming down on one polemical side or another. So I worry that people take what you say and then exaggerate it beyond recognition, and then in turn blame you for not going far enough with what you're saying. It's easy to appear weak if you're not being extremist and polemical. I think that that is often the case, and that the person who is being careful is really being strong.

'I think the people who are using ornament are extremely confused. Much of what's being done is dominated by aesthetics, and of course that's wrong, because the functional quality is important as well. And the danger is that the current emphasis on history is a symptom that architects are forgetting the social side of architecture and planning.

'We used to be called right wing because we designed for rich clients. Then we were called left wing because we looked at Las Vegas and the architecture of the lower middle class, and that meant that we were allied with the politics of the people like that, and it wasn't necessarily the case. Architects have to accommodate different taste cultures. They can't say there's one taste – my upper-middle-class taste – which I'm trying to impose on all the landscape. The landscape has to connect with combinations of taste cultures, and that's something that interests us very much. In other words, working with clients who do not have our tastes or our sophistication. It's a very interesting subject and full of ironies because, in the end, the lower economic classes really do want to ape middle-class forms and take on the values of middle-class people.'

Robert Venturi's own work has done the opposite – it has used irony to introduce vernacular forms to upper-class people. His buildings exaggerate common-or-garden features which simultaneously serve a functional purpose and a symbolic purpose while subverting the convention that they spring from. This is legitimate, he says, because it is a response both to the spirit of the age, and to his own predilections, but it should stay within limits and recognise that it must still be capable of being read by the unsophisticated.

'Mannerism is not the only approach, and there can be problems of becoming too esoteric, but it's an approach which I and others have felt at home in and I think it's a reflection of the ambiguity of our time. For instance, at the beginning of this century, you could be Bernard "Sure" [Shaw] – you could be a very strong artist and take unambiguous stands. The good guys and the bad guys – it was obvious who they were. Now, I think, intelligent people are no longer that sure of simple answers and drastic actions, and this is reflected in the fact that there are inevitable contradictions and ambiguities in the work. I think our approach has been that we make a strong statement but then we say, OK, this statement or this order can be broken.'

How close does this come to answering the question of whether civilisation is being brought to the brink of chaos by the forces of reaction? The problem is that the idea of dismantling a style and reassembling it is a modern idea, and one which could only occur to a modern architect trained to regard architecture as a rational discipline, and conscious that he is abusing – or having fun with – its rational objectives. It does not exist in the repertory of traditional architecture, nor does it suggest that architects have moved backwards into historical modes of thought, even if they have clad their thinking in eccentrically old-fashioned clothing. At the same time, it does not make them any closer to establishing a rapport with the public, which was one of their principal aims. Less so, perhaps, since one has to know the game of architecture to understand how irony bridges the gap between the appearance of the building and the intentions which lie behind it. To that extent, what appears to be a mood of revivalism is not a revival at all.

Robert Venturi goes further. 'Many of the people who [around 1970] were violent Modernists, doing all those white buildings in the style of the 1920s, are now taking up historicism and being anti-Modern. In order to progress, everybody has to react against the older generation. I was doing it. But I don't think that means that you have to hate your father in order to love your grandfather. I think that's very unhealthy, and we've stated this a number of times: that we admire and very much come out of the Modern Movement, and that everything we're doing now is an evolution from the Modern Movement. So when we criticise it, we're not criticising all of it – just the later corruption. And I think we'll all be very much better architects if we are more understanding of where we come from, and not so fanatical about being different from the immediate past.'

Some architects, like Robert Venturi, have used the revival as a way of distancing themselves from the unacceptable face of Modernism, without actually relinquishing any of the beliefs that underlie it. Others have adopted alternatives to twentieth-century theory, apparently unaware of the similarity in structure, if not in content, of the ideology they have taken on. Jeremy Dixon, however, has now moved away from the Mannerism of his earlier work towards a more conservative reconciliation with history. In his housing scheme in Maida Vale, he has allowed himself to be far more literal about the sources he quoted from than at North Kensington five years earlier. It's not a direction he could have predicted then. But he has found in the revival the opportunity to question his approach to architecture, and learn to be more true to himself. It has been a period of coming out.

'I'm not proposing that this way of working is the bright hope of the future, but rather a kind of rearguard action for the moment. That is, if you're confronted with cities in a state of disarray, your first move is not necessarily to propose a new, radical way of doing things but to take a step backwards, to reassess, and to see which moves look surest. So I find it difficult to say this way of thinking is visionary. It's just a way of operating now.'

Digging Graves

Michael Graves is an architect of perversity. His mind is extremely intelligent, extremely artistic, and extremely original, and he wishes his architecture to be the same way too. The product is a scholasticism so eccentric that it can be compared with Giulio Romano and the early sixteenth-century Italian Mannerists. Like them, his sources are conservative but his manner outrageous. He stands in a similar relationship to his culture; he is a Counter-Reformationist, hostile to what has just been, overstating his relationship with what was there before.

Graves was born in Indianapolis in 1934, studying at Cincinnati University and then at Harvard. After taking his master's in 1959, he won the Prix de Rome and spent two years studying art and architecture in Italy. On his return to the USA in 1962, he took up a teaching post at Princeton University, an election which predated any professional experience of architecture as a practical skill. He is now Princeton's Schriner Professor. His architecture has therefore always existed within a narrow academic context.

His work is more familiar on the page than on the building site. Of forty-seven projects carried out between 1964, when he set up in practice, and 1981, less than half were brought to completion, and of those, only seven were new buildings, the rest being re-furbishments, interior designs, exhibition spaces, or additions to existing buildings. He has had greater success with his drawings which are now highly valuable and highly collected on the New York art market. His hesitant line and his use of warm pastels have served to launder his freakish imagery, making him a magazine celebrity (there were over 130 write-ups about him by 1980), keeping his name and house-style in the public eye, and winning him over forty architectural awards.

His designs represent a reaction against the social preoccu-pations of the 1950s and 60s. They are a move back into the self. His buildings do not want to change the world; they barely know the world exists. What they do know is *the-artist-as-genius* and *architecture-as-history*. These two themes combine to provide him with an arcane and private set of rules.

In his early work, Graves immersed himself in the idealised art movements of post-First World War France, taking from Cubism for his architecture and from Purism for his murals and decorative work. These he reprocessed to make them more quintessential, more active, more intense. His general direction was similar to that of four other American architects – Peter Eisenman, Charles Gwathmey, John Hejduk and Richard Meier. All these men shared an interest in Le Corbusier's exploration of geometrical themes: abstract form, space, intersections, the grid, the corner, the plane, the curve, the line, the point – taking to an extreme the paradox of using abstraction in order to be more rather than less complex. They became known as the New York Five – or The Whites, on the strength of their Cubist references – although they never worked together as a group.

Their work challenged the spectator – or more often, the reader – to follow their coded references, their symbolic rela-tionships, the significance of colour. Everything meant *something*, and possibly *something else* as well. This was architecture for crossword fanatics; Graves may only have been *The Times* to Eisenman's *Ximenes* but it was still flattering to be able to make sense of what he offered.

In his earliest building – the Hanselmann House of 1967 – Graves was already painting fragmented Purist murals on the walls – work in the style of Ozenfant and Gris. As the decorative interest grew, conditioned perhaps by the number of commissions he was receiving for interiors, so his appetite for colour and imagery grew more dominant. Abstraction became a decorative form in itself, with diagonally-laid trellises and complicated geometrical pergolas being used to break down his buildings into three-dimensional collages. It was as if Braque and Picasso had been locked up in a room with Rietveld and Mondrian and left to fight it out.

Around 1977, the work took a new turn, clutching at a new set of purist forms gathered from antiquity in addition to the earlier geometrical ones: the headstone, the round arch, the templum, the pyramid, the truncated pyramid, the pediment, the portico, the post, the column, paired columns, the colonnade, the pylon, the step, the stair, the ball, the poplar tree. It was like a replay of the 1930s – a degeneration from Modernism into Art Deco.

Hand in hand with the new forms went formulas for their treatment: giantism, super-simplicity, exaggerated proportions (excessive length or excessive squatness), physiognomic symmetry, dramatic asymmetry, mechanical repetition, distortion, negative shapes, intensely contrasted surface treatments – large areas of plain stucco set off against rustication and marbling.

Graves' new directions were received with excitement among America's younger intellectual coterie of architects – especially by the critic Charles Jencks who promoted him as the figurehead of his own campaign for 'Post-Modernism'. In particular, Jencks pinned his hopes on Graves' cubic office block for the city administration in Portland, Oregon, which although it got built – in the face of widespread opposition – was not completed as either of them had wished. Graves' other most notable recent work has been the headquarters of the Humana Corporation in Louisville, Kentucky – a building which, characteristically, combines the monumentalism of Baalbek with the exquisiteness of Art Deco and the clumsiness of Toytown.

Graves' showrooms for Sunar, the fabric and furniture company, his furniture for the Italian designers Memphis, his shopping bags for Bloomingdale's and his other experiments in home decoration have led to his being called an interior designer rather than an architect – a label he strongly rejects, as if cerebral complexity provided all designers with an automatic safety net. The problem is, what is the quality of that complexity?

In furnishing new relationships between the previously unconnected, Graves stimulates the power of association. But there comes a point where the relating of things unlike turns into contradiction. In his work, symbolic massiveness is contradicted by the thinness of its materials. Nice joke. But there are also contradictions between its playful intentions and its restlessness, between its profundity and its preciosity. These cannot all be of equal value, nor can they all have been intended. So how does one distinguish between good contradictions and bad ones, between good associations and bad ones? How does the mind of a Mannerist work?

Graves: I suspect that over the last ten years, I've been simply trying to say two things. First, that my work is abstract by nature because of the geometric compositions that I use, and that it can therefore risk being very obscure in terms of the layman. But at the same time, it has to be figurative enough to allow the layman to participate in it. Then again, the ambiguities of abstraction can have secondary and tertiary meanings that you might not have with a fully figurative proposition or narrative.

Certainly, the work has changed in the last twenty years from abstraction to figuration. I was very taken by critical evaluation of my work in the early 6os. People would say to me that they thought I was speaking a private language – a language, as you say, that was bound in Purism and the abstractions of Le Corbusier and the Modern Movement, and that though the work was intriguing in terms of light and shadow, and its formal composition, it nevertheless was mute in terms of figurative accessibility.

Games: Let me hold you up on that point. We know what's meant by figuration in painting but what does figuration mean in architecture?

Graves: There is in architecture a kind of miming, as if we had a chance to look at a building and the building somehow looks back at us. For instance, a building might have a base that roots it in the ground and gives it a certain stability. It has a body as we do – a centre, in other words – and it generally has a top or a head. The base is the basement. Above that we have the *piano nobile*. And above that, the attic, which is the most private because it's the furthest from the street. And therefore we assign bedrooms to that level, while living rooms and dining rooms might be in the *piano nobile*, and service might be in the basement. That kind of attribution of activity to the composition of the building starts to suggest a miming of our own bodily condition.

We also think of that figurative sense in terms of the theme of a building. If I say to you that the floor of this room is like the ground, you can believe it more quickly than if I say it's like the sky. However, if I say the soffit of the ceiling is like the sky, especially after we've seen a Tiepolo ceiling painting, we think of lightness – of lifting the lid off a building. The wall can also be painted like a landscape. So that you get from the floor to the wall of green with its landscape beyond, to ultimately the celestial soffit. And so there again is that figurative sense giving thematic content to buildings. And the modern architect – not myself, but others – might make the whole thing devoid of that thematic reference, and therefore ability to have access to it is lessened.

Games: So it's conventionality that you've been striving for?

Graves: In that sense, yes. I think the figurative language is broad enough, once that thematic reference is set, to say many things. But if I paint the whole room white or grey, I can only speak of modern abstraction.

Games: What you've done there is to describe the traditional building. If you're going back to that, why do you find it necessary to use a language of description that is so unfamiliar and arcane?

Graves: I think it's terribly familiar. One of my interests is to make the familiarity of my work such that society can get into it. I think there is lots to say once you have access to the work. Look at the difference between Piero della Francesca and Fra Angelico. It's enormous. But the technique of description is very similar, and one would not mistake the one for other. But the themes, the stories, the text, are quite divergent in what they try to say.

Games: Isn't it the other way round? The imagery you use in your work is very similar to Juan Gris and Baumeister and all those people who were producing paintings and collages in the 1920s and 30s. They had none of the preoccupations with meaning and structuralism that you have. Why do you need those preoccupations?

Graves: I wish I believed that but I believe just the opposite. Braque and Gris and Picasso in his best days were certainly talking about the relationship between the forms of daily use – the artefacts of anything from the kitchen to the table – and how they were used formally in terms of painting, as well as for what they could say about the *Zeitgeist*, the spirit of the day. All of that was there through a kind of sexual description – certainly in Gris' work. Remember, those paintings were being painted about the time Freud was writing *The Interpretation of Dreams* and the relationship is terribly clear between one and the other. They picked up the prosaic artefacts of daily use and used them in the most sublime way.

Games: So would you agree that your work is part of a tradition of *critical* art, of *critical* architecture, rather than *artist's* art or *architect's* architecture?

Graves: Yes, but in the best sense they are one and the same thing. To say 'architect's art' or 'architect's architecture' suggests that one is speaking a private language and that one speaks only to the *cognoscenti* – only those who would pick up the clues. Certainly, in architecture as in painting or music, there are varieties of readings. If I were a musician and very skilled at my craft, I'd get more out of Mozart than a layman would – my life would be enriched by understanding the deep structure of the music – though as a layman not trained in music, Mozart would nevertheless be accessible to me on one level.

The same can be said of architecture, although it is still current in architectural thinking that this should not be the case – that all architecture should be, as we say in America, 'up front': everything accessible in a populist language. I don't think that's right. I think that the building of architecture, the making of an enclosure, certainly should not work against the inhabitants as it does in many cases; that's to be deplored. But at the same time, looking at work by James Stirling would be enriched by having a knowledge of Palladio or Vitruvius or the culture of architecture. There's no getting around it. The more we know about the history of any art, the richer the references might be.

Games: You became a professor at Princeton University in 1962. You hadn't yet built anything then. What pressures did your academic post put your architecture under?

Graves: I hadn't built anything, except in working for other people in other offices. I was a kid. To turn the question round, my undergraduate training and my graduate training at Harvard left me feeling pretty dumb, coming into the world of architecture. Having won awards, I suppose I was doing it as well as my peers, but I still felt untrained. I felt not that I'd simply have to go back to school but that I wasn't critically ready for what I thought my potential might be. More reading and more looking was necessary. So just before arriving at Princeton I spent two years at the American Academy in Rome and spent almost every day either in the city looking at buildings or drawing them – I think I made two thousand drawings in my two years there – or in the library. And that got the juices flowing. I knew that in that awakening that Rome gave me, not that I was home but that I was on my way to constructing an academic life for myself, or at least a critical life if I didn't stay in the university. I never planned to stay in the university twenty-one years, as I have done. I thought I'd get a practice started by virtue of being able to teach part-time. It didn't work out that way. I taught full-time for many years and did competitions with Princeton colleagues and finally started to get small commissions. I was known for years as 'The Cubist Kitchen King' because I was only given minute commissions in and around Princeton. It's only in recent years that I've enjoyed any kind of large-scale work.

Games: What burden does a working architect holding a major academic post carry with him?

Graves: I don't know how it works in Britain but in the United States there is a very negative feeling towards academics. I was given a rather prestigious award a few years ago by the American Academy and Institute of Arts and Letters. The architect who presented me with it had nothing to do with my selection and felt in fact that *he* was under pressure because he was the controlling partner of Skidmore Owings and Merrill, the largest architectural firm in the world.[1]

There is a sense that the best builders are the macho guys that kick a building every day and don't think about it too much, but just get it built. And the cruder you can be about it, the closer you get to the bricklayer or the contractor. Often times those people are just the opposite – they're good at their craft and think quite deliberately about it. But there is a sense that writers, critics, academics – those who are verbal, those who are able even to draw their architecture – may not be able to build. And I think that a number of us are now turning that around. Certainly, firms like Skidmore Owings and Merrill are having second thoughts now that many of us are winning competitions and getting major commissions, and their work starts to look more like ours every day. This is not so healthy. But nevertheless, as people start to retire and our students start to enter those large firms, the balance of critical evaluation of our work changes.

[1]The occasion was May 1980, the award was the Arnold W. Brunner Memorial Prize for Architecture, and the architectural statesman at the ceremony was Gordon Bunshaft, who remarked cryptically from the rostrum before sitting down: 'We used to give prizes to architects for doing buildings. Now we give prizes to architects for drawing pictures.'

The real question is: How can students who have been in academia for five or six years then go out from the university and sit at a drawing board and evaluate their work? That's what it's all about. It's very lonely out there if you're working by yourself or even in a large firm, and you have no one to talk to about what you're doing. You have to have made a path into the evaluation of your work during your time at university.

Games: The opposite may apply, that one can become too self-conscious and too introspective. Has that bothered you?

Graves: No, it may have bothered other people looking at my work, but it's not bothered me.

Games: You don't find that the academic world becomes too introspective?

Graves: Oh, it can.

Games: And too self-regarding?

Graves: Certainly, one could lay that claim to academia in very much the same way as I've just been suggesting that the professional world does – in exactly the same terms of just plain good ol' boys building without thinking. Either is possible, and one tries to keep a balance. I go back to the Mozart analogy and say that I want to be tuneful and say something that is accessible and upfront. At the same time, I want to allow the density of my intentions to be understood by those that will.

Games: You talked about being in Rome for two years. Of course, all artists for five hundred years have gone to Rome, and sometimes what they learn from Rome is oblique. They may come back and try to educate or uplift the public. Le Corbusier and his generation came back to *épater le bourgeois*. But you're not doing that, are you? You're doing something rather different.

Graves: Well, I don't know. People criticise me for looking back to the past – for using historical references. I would love to be able to use only archetypal references, because I think that's the basis of the myth and ritual of architecture. But I get primarily that language from Rome – that kind of continuous language. I see architecture as a cultural continuity and parts – but not all – of modern architecture are an appendage to that. It's like atonal music, it's a way of inverting the language. And, yes, I'm saying that there is an accessible language which is so broadly based as to be almost everything *but* inversion.

For instance, if Michelangelo had used a palette of colours in his buildings that would have given us thematic acccess to them, and if red or terracotta or brown were used to weight the building, to give it base and to suggest stability, and if light blue or azure blue were used, as I said earlier, to describe the soffit or the ceiling, we as a society would understand that in an almost subliminal way. However, if a de Stijl architect, or in some cases a Modern architect, uses blue abstractly, it means only blue. It does not mean sky, it does not mean water. Red means red, blue means blue, and black means black. And that's the way that Mondrian and Rietveld and other painters and architects used colour – without a reference system.

It's very difficult to look at Mondrian's 'Broadway Boogie-Woogie' and not think about the colours as having a reference system in a way we have always known in a childlike or subliminal fashion to describe or understand our landscape. But those artists were working directly against the grain, as it were, to suggest that colours and form had no reference in anything past, present, or future. And that describes – for me, at least – an internalised and private system, a system that the man on the street simply won't get. And that's what I'm working directly against.

Games: You're working towards an architecture which is going to be more familiar to the man on the street?

Graves: Exactly.

Games: Would you recognise that while attempting to do that, your buildings are consistently eccentric?

Graves: They are indeed eccentric. I think they probably try too much. I've been without work for so long that I'm probably over-anxious and trying to say too much. But now that there is an abundance of work, I'm a little more patient with myself, in the sense that I know that the phone will ring tomorrow and I will get another commission and this probably won't be my last commission. And therefore the rheostat won't be turned up quite so high, and the eccentricities might be normalised.

But there are eccentric architects like Sir Edwin Lutyens who make buildings both for the common man and for me. And so all the ranges between black and white, all the grey ranges, are somehow for me satisfied in a Lutyens composition.

Games: But what about the needs of the building? In what way is the architectural language that you've developed equally appropriate for the Humana Corporation in Kentucky as it is for the Matsuya Ginza Department Store in Japan?

Graves: Whether we're oriental or from Kentucky, similar kinds of situations occur in both cultures. There is a sense of what Le Corbusier calls 'the architectural promenade' – of knowing the kind of space you're about to encounter, or that you are encountering as you move through the building in terms of its placement, its height, its enclosure, its light, the way it relates to its neighbouring space.

What you're suggesting is that an oriental culture thinks in a dramatically different way from us. But for good or for not, the westernisation of Tokyo is quite extensive. It looks to me as much like Des Moines as anywhere else. Very curious things are going on. The city was essentially rebuilt after 1940 and it is not very attractive. In fact, the people at Matsuya on Ginza, the main shopping street of Tokyo, had asked me to make a monument to the commercial life of Japan. I found it a very curious request and certainly the building has similarities with the one in Kentucky, in the hierarchical assemblage of rooms and spaces. But it is, I think, somewhat different in that while the Matsuya Ginza store is inspired in part by the stone monuments of Japan and there is a similarly based body and head with anthropomorphic associations, there is a weight and gravity to that building that doesn't occur, for me at least, in the Humana Building in Louisville, Kentucky.

Games: I'd say that whatever use you might have made of local Japanese architecture is so stylised that it almost doesn't matter. It's rather like International Modernism: your buildings look the same wherever they happen to be. Each brief seems like an opportunity to explore your own architecture rather than an architecture suggested by your client. Which is strange, given that conventional Modernism is what you're dead set against.

Graves: Well, there is in any language, and certainly in architecture, a general language. That's what I meant before in talking about thematic reference, anthropomorphic reference, without ever being historical. At the same time, there must be a specific language. The Humana Building, for example, would be very awkwardly placed in any other location in that city. There are five- or six-storey Victorian storefronts adjacent to the building and because of that, I've employed a reference to a loggia or colonnade in the building and on the face of the building, and hoped that the point will be caught that there is a similarity. However, our building is much taller and therefore there is a gradual build-up of scale from the neighbouring buildings to the final height of our building. There is also an enormous waterfall within the loggia of our building which looks back to the Ohio river. Louisville was founded on the Falls of the Ohio, and so you see the rushing of that river at that particular place. And on the face of the building that looks across the river to the state of Indiana, I have an enormous upper-level porch that hangs out over the building in a lyrical form similar to the lyricism of the river. Now, given access to that porch, one can have lunch there, one can look out over the river, can get the breeze, can get the light. Again, though one might find another site for those various references and activities, they do become more specific to Louisville and that particular site than to somewhere else. So there's where my 'take' on architecture – general and specific – becomes localised to the site.

Games: That seems like a tactical response to the brief, hunting for an accumulation of local references to justify what amounts to architectural indulgence. It's very Walt Whitman. But how do your interests in anthropomorphism, for example, serve the interests of your client?

Graves: It gives access to the work. It's so curious that Modernism has taught us that there is only one access to work – Functionalism. Walter Gropius drilled it into us to the point that we talk about architecture as a functional art, and that architecture isn't architecture unless it's functional. But in a way, we were sold a bill of goods, because that was only half the story. If there is a pragmatic functionalism, there is at the same time a symbolic functionalism. And it serves the interests of the client to have access to his architecture and his spaces by virtue of the symbolism that is there.

For instance, the door is encased in a frame and one passes over a threshold. The man in the street knows what a threshold is as well as the architect. The architect might, if he's instructing the builder how to make it, call it a door cill. And therein lies the difference between the pragmatic response and the symbolic response. If I married tomorrow and carried my bride over the *door cill*, she'd ask me: 'Dear Michael, let's go back and try it again. You know, that's not the way the poet has asked us to perform this rite. I'd very much like to be carried over the *threshold* into our room.' It is in that act that we are acting both in the interests of the client to keep the rain off, and to give him a chance to have the structure of composition around the myths and rituals that this society has indeed invented. The architect didn't invent them. We as a culture invented the necessity for a threshold or the necessity for a window or a door. The idea of decoration on a wall – it's pure invention; we don't have to have it in a pragmatic sense. But it might be said that our lives would not be terribly rich without it in a symbolic sense.

Games: Of course, much of the excitement in this century has concerned the examining of these myths and discovering that they are empty.

Graves: They're not for me, and I hope they're not for the rest. My life is terribly rich because they're alive and well. As you and I sit here looking at each other, we are at the same time engaged in a rite of conversation. We are face to face. And indeed, if we were back to back, I wouldn't be able to see whether you were grimacing and doubting what I was saying or smiling and accepting it. All of that interchange in that miming act that architecture and man go through is terribly important to me. We sit here in these two chairs with both of us at this moment with our legs crossed. If there had been a table between us, we might not have crossed our legs. It's quite clear in a Freudian sense why our legs are crossed. And that again is playing out a rite. And I think it is part of architecture – playing out a daily action. I mean, we do these things and as long as these acts are with us, the myths and rituals we've invented will be with us as well. My life isn't empty, it's quite full. I can't wait to get up tomorrow morning.

Games: Thinking of Gordon Bunshaft and the AAIAL awards ceremony, you are known not just for your architecture but for your architectural drawings which command extremely high prices now in the salerooms of New York. How happy are you with the way your drawings translate into buildings on the ground?

Graves: My answer to you will be unsatisfactory, I suspect, because we think that there is an immediate translation of drawing to building. That of course doesn't happen in painting. We look at a painting by Piero della Francesca and we think about the liturgy or the text as well as simply the technique and composition. But in architecture, we think of something else; we think about translation from the act of drawing to the building itself. But remember, the architect has gone through another act before putting it on paper. He's already had a series of ideas about architecture that he's had to translate to the drawing. And so there's already a gap between the thought and the drawing, as there is a gap between the drawing and the building.

Now that gap may be something that disturbs you in that sometimes my drawings don't look like my buildings, because what I'm trying to suggest in the drawing is an act of participation in the life of the work and its critical evaluation, that I hope will be similar in the room or space or building itself. That's not to say that I'm not able to portray the look of that building in my drawing. What I want to try and get across is the conceptual stance, rather than what my building will look like in the rain, or that on a sunny day there will be a baby carriage and a mum walking the child in front of it to give it some sense of scale. I want the building to give the scale of reference, and so if I leave a person out of the drawing of my building, it is in the hope that the building will suggest how big *we* are, rather than for a person to show how big *it* is.

But I would also say that a drawing is a drawing and a building is a building and I don't ask my buildings to look like my drawings any more than I ask my drawings to look like my buildings. However, I would be quick to say that I hope there is a conceptual similarity between the two and if I've missed that then I've missed the point of the drawing – or maybe you have – but I suspect that I would go back to the drawing board if you were to say to me: 'No, I don't get it, Michael. Try it again.' I would indeed try it again.

Games: You draw extensively and you clearly enjoy drawing and making pretty things. I wonder whether you really are a drawer, or a painter, who only happens to be involved in making architectural forms.

Graves: Well, yes, I like doing beautiful things – that's the greatest gift. If you say I do that, I will take the compliment.

Games: I said 'pretty' rather than 'beautiful'!

Graves: Yes, I said 'beautiful', didn't I? If you want to put it in the pejorative, you can. If you want to say that my things are not beautiful, say that; be direct. You know, I don't know what 'pretty' is. I clearly do enjoy drawing. I clearly enjoy building and it should not be assumed that because I draw, I enjoy building less. Gordon Bunshaft, my critic when I received the award, clearly does not draw. I don't know if for Gordon Bunshaft it is not a manly act or it's not a building act, but can you imagine Michelangelo or Borromini or Bernini or Vitruvius not drawing? I mean, how in the world would you ever describe in architecture without drawing it? You can do it by models, that's a three-dimensional description which I do as much as drawing. A drawing's a two-dimensional description. But you know, nobody's interested in buying a Gordon Bunshaft or a Skidmore Owings and Merrill drawing; in a way they don't exist. They of course exist but they exist as technical artefacts. They aren't artefacts that involve the conceptual act, and how terribly boring it must be to get up every morning and go to the drawing board and make these bloody awful descriptions of bricks and mortar that have dimensions on them, without ever imagining what the conceptual basis for the work is. I would imagine that that immediately flies in the face of the Modern architect who has not drawn for at least fifty years, although it seems like a millennium, in the way that many many architects have drawn for the last three thousand years. But there are architects like myself who are drawing again, making models, and making a conceptual architecture that we hope will be translated into building form.

Games: One expects an architect to have a natural sense of the three-dimensional and the sculptural, but one doesn't necessarily expect him or her to be able to draw, and in fact it might be a division of aspirations to draw and build.

Graves: I don't see that. I didn't say 'draw well'; I don't care if you draw with your elbows. Draw any way you want to draw, but you have to put it down. You have to be able to describe what you're going to do. If you're going to write a piece, you have to write it down to see how the words connect, to see how the semantic dimension is attuned to the syntax and your thoughts. Tell me another way.

Games: You wouldn't agree that for architects who think in a very painterly way, there may be scope for self-delusion?

Graves: There may be. I'd rather have that than not.

Games: I'm thinking of those Victorian architects – Scott, Burges, Waterhouse, and their contemporaries – whose drawings are so prized at the moment. Perhaps their drawings are prized because it is in the drawings that they really achieved their architectural goals rather than in their buildings.

Graves: You really think so? I'm rather charmed by their buildings, as I am with Palladio's drawings and buildings, even Scamozzi's drawings of Palladio's buildings. What you're I think suggesting is that there might be a romantic tendency in a drawing that is never realised in a building, and what I'm trying to get across is that there is a conceptual act to drawing and that that should be portrayed in the act of building as well. If we miss it, then we miss it. But if we never imagined it in the first place, how in the world are we ever going to make a conceptual building or an intention in the building that's involved with the ideas that enrich our culture? I have no idea.

Games: Well, I look at your Public Services Building in Portland, Oregon, and I see a fifteen-storey cube with paintings on the side and not a lot of sculpture and not a lot of sense of three-dimensional articulation.

Graves: There you're absolutely right. The building is terribly flat, and there you are clearly the critic and not the builder because, I don't know whether it's true in this country but I'm sure it's true world-wide, the sculpture you're asking for – the depth of the façade, the chiaroscuro, requires a construction technique that allows for recession and advancement of the wall plane and, my dear, that is very expensive. We're talking about a building that is $50 per square foot which in America is next to nothing. We can't build housing for that, and this is what we call a speculative office building. It is very very flat and I have portrayed on the façade that same life of the plane inside the building as one progresses within the architectural promenade of hierarchical, spatial identification. I've tried to make a building that will be as rich in its flatness – yes, in a painterly way – as a building which is literally deep.

Now indeed, that relationship existed before Rome and Pompeii, and the Romans certainly in the Golden House of Nero were able to make a three-dimensional art made of the finest marbles and materials. In Pompeii, a society that had only brains and not the money to make a sculptural articulation of the type you're talking about, they painted it on, and we are richer today because we have the flat surface of a Pompeian wall. Also, the urbanistic configuration of a Pompeian house restricted their ability to poke a hole in the wall, to make a window, because they were cheek by jowl with the next building. And so they got central light in the *atrium*, and they painted the wall in such a way that you saw the garden through the painter's eye. Of course it was an imitation garden it was a *trompe l'oeil* garden, it was *faux*ed surface, but it was just that artform that occurred over a 79-year stretch that made us understand the full range of Pompeian painting, and by the time the mountain blew up, the folks up north in Rome were so engaged by these painters that they started to paint on their surfaces as well, and it became an act of human and artistic intervention that was then copied by Romans who could well have afforded to build the real thing instead of the illusion. They decided it was a higher act to do that.

Well I'm not suggesting that. I'm only suggesting that there might be a necessity for us to have access into the depth of the building, and we're so attuned to the shadow that we want that I'm certainly willing to paint it or in this case put it on with tile and paint and other materials in a way that would encourage a depth which the budget of the building wouldn't allow. I'll be happy to paint it on any day.

Games: If there is an apparent depth and richness and illusion on the exterior of the building, the interior seems far more Beaux Arts and conventional – highly symmetrical plans that are so concerned with geometry that the spaces have no obvious sense of their own. They're more like forests of geometrically disposed columns.

Graves: Obviously I think just the opposite. The open plan of Le Corbusier or the free plan of Mies van der Rohe is actually the same thing. It was invented to allow us the freedom to put the wall anywhere. What Le Corbusier made was a series of columns or points supporting the floor above. That allowed us to put the walls in positions they were formerly not able to enjoy, and I have frequently used a system like Corbusier's Maison Dom-Ino.

However, that is not to say that all my spaces are asymmetrical or symmetrical. They're certainly not. Look at one of my buildings and you will see symmetries where they are useful and asymmetries where they are useful, and the differences are clarified generally by the specifics of the site – for instance, between the symmetry of the site that we have in Portland, Oregon, for the Portland Public Services Building, as against the asymmetrical site that we have in Louisville, Kentucky. The corner site there is made explicit in the plan. But I'm encouraged enough to think that by the contrast of free plans and free associations of plans and my inability to find my way in many modern buildings – as against what you call Beaux-Arts buildings (I don't think I'm a Beaux-Arts planner) – there is more order to my plans than there is in late Le Corbusier plans.

Games: Sure, but when you're forced into having to have a particular sized room on one side of the building just to balance one on the other side of the building, because you happen to be interested in symmetries, it suggests that geometry is more important than the use the building is serving. How does that enrich the building?

Graves: Oh, I would agree with you. But that doesn't happen in my buildings. I would certainly use balance if that seemed appropriate to a given sequence of spaces or rooms, but I wouldn't balance a square room on one side with a square room on the other if it were inappropriate to the use. The floor plan of the Humana Corporation, for example, has balance in its central motif – there is a measure of symmetry to the lobby – but it has entries which occur on certain sides that don't occur on the other.

Games: One of the features of American commercial architecture is the premium it puts on novelty and self-promotion. Where does the commercial element come into your work?

Graves: I was told by a developer recently that he was hiring architect X because architect Y had recently made a building nearby and the building that was being built at that time was receiving so much press that he had somehow to be more outrageous. I found it a most curious comment. I was not hired by that developer – I don't know how one would ever sustain that kind of upping the ante every time. It seems quite mad to me. I've never been engaged in that, never been asked by a developer to be outrageous or to do something in contrast to somebody else's work simply to rent more offices. But it does happen. I don't know whether it happens in Britain or not[1] but it happens every day in the United States.

Games: It might be said that in developer's language, you were an outrageous architect, and attractive for that very reason.

Graves: No, in fact as you said at the start, I'm quite orthodox.

Games: I also said you were eccentric.

Graves: I suppose within the specific elements of my buildings there are eccentric elements. But I don't think the overall building forms are in any sense outrageous. A lot of people do. I don't read them that way. I don't tilt the tops, and I don't make steel and glass reflective architecture. I don't make outrageous statements about buildings in that sense.

Games: You build gigantic portals – think of the Plocek House –

[1] It does not. Office developers in this country compete with each other to be bashful.

and you flirt with bad taste. You take forms and exaggerate them. These would seem to be techniques of self-exhibition of a kind that parallels the self-exhibition required by developers.

Graves: I don't do those things to attract attention at all. If I made a door or a portal too big, I would scold myself and make it smaller next time, and you in a way attribute too much to a knowledge of exactly what I'm going to do before I do it. I mean, I made the drawing and I made the model and I thought that the portal was properly scaled, let's say, in the Plocek House. If I had to do it over again I would probably reduce the scale. I would turn the rheostat down maybe 10 or 15 per cent. I missed by that much, but that's what practice is about, I suppose.

Games: For the reasons we've talked about, it might be that people appreciate your work for trivial or meretricious reasons. Does that bother you?

Graves: I don't know why they appreciate the work. I can't get into their skins. All I can do is be a part of the society that feels a certain way towards architecture. Obviously if enough people said to me that they didn't like my work, that it's a private language, and that I should try it again, I probably would. One wants to do well. I'm not so convinced that I have the only take on it, and if there were enough negative criticism – and I can tell you, there's a lot! – I might do something. But there's enough positive as well to keep me going. I listen and I suppose I'm vulnerable in that way. My skin doesn't seem to get any thicker.

I recently went to our national architects' convention, and there were people there wearing buttons, wearing badges, that said: 'I don't dig Graves.' And they had the international symbol for non-entry pasted across a picture of the front door of the Portland Building. I mean, it gets you down.

A Magnificent Catastrophe

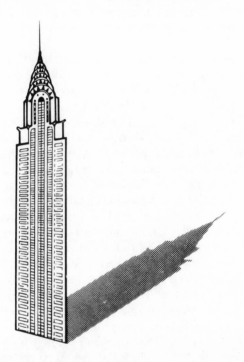

When the Catalan composer Manuel de Falla was a child, he used to hide himself in a tiny wardrobe in his bedroom and transport himself to an imaginary city of his own inventing. He made up a population and a government to go with the city, made paper money for them to spend and train tickets for them to buy. It seemed harmless enough, but what started off as an absorbing game became an obsession – at least in the eyes of his parents, who feared for his sanity. Finally, to save the child, they destroyed the city by destroying all the tokens of its existence.

The idea of the city as an invention of the human mind is a threatening thing. The city is the domain of man – a symbol of artifice, and a challenge to Nature. God stops at the city gate, leaving man to rule over a miniature cosmos that is neither natural nor divine. In Biblical times, the accidental crime of manslaughter was punishable by banishment to one of four cities of exile; but in a sense, all cities are cities of exile, and have been ever since the crime in the Garden of Eden, for before the first crime there were no cities.

The city is therefore the reward but also the penalty for the exercise of human will; it is a place where the ungodly become gods. And for that arrogance, the city becomes a place where the stitches of human ambitions forever come apart. Generations of poets have warned that the city is a flawed, fragile, impermanent thing.

Cities are complex and contradictory. The more duplication that exists, the more we see unity. Where there are many people, we see not the individuals but a crowd or the Public. Where there are many cars, we see Traffic. To talk about the city at all, we have to name single things. The biggest single thing we can name in the city is the city itself. To name smaller things, we have to be able to isolate them from the backgrounds into which they melt. That means selecting. For our convenience, we may go to writers who have already done the job of selecting for us. For us, Berlin is always Isherwood's Berlin; Paris is Hemingway's Paris. For the Russians, London is Dickens' London. Because cities are artificial things, they lend themselves to interpretation and to myth.

The myths by which one understands a city can change, however. In the fifteenth and sixteenth centuries, mercantile Venice was jealously viewed by an aspirant England as a symbol of wealth and stable government. As the fortunes of the two empires crossed, so Venice became a metaphor for less desirable qualities – licentiousness and political treachery, then corruption and impotence. In the eyes of Turner and Ruskin it had become the epitome of Romantic melancholy; to Mann, it was death. At every step, Venetians seem to have acquiesced in the judgements made about them, to the point that the idea of decline developed its own self-fulfilling inertia. By contrast, the act of founding a city is easy; it is an act of the imagination. It does not yet know what its problems are going to be. The difficult thing is keeping the city going once it has been founded, for that defies the imagination. God's revenge.

All matter proceeds to decay, unless there is a constant flow of energy through it. Many of the prettiest English market towns rose to power as cathedral cities on the back of the church. The great agricultural towns of the west of England grew rich on wool. The industrial north exploited its resources of coal and iron ore. But each has subsequently declined. The crown usurped the power of the church; international trade undercut the wool market; central government drew economic activity away to the south.

The energy that had kept these towns strong and then abandoned them was that of economic power, for all powerful economies have started out weak and had to fight for their position. The power of the Venetian city state lay in its lack of resources; it started out a loser. It had to take imaginative risks; it had to invent advantages over its better established rivals. And this is the rule: there are no such things as natural resources in the physical world; there are only natural disadvantages. The only natural resource is the idea that converts a disadvantage into an asset.

But ideas can work both ways, and it is tempting to see the same process of maturation and decay that affects human life affecting human institutions. Gibbon used the Romans to express his anxiety that society might be locked into an inevitable process of decline. Vasari was haunted by the fear that after the climax of Michelangelo, art had nothing more than old age to look forward to. If Gibbon and Vasari were right, we had better learn to grow old gracefully. But if decline is only a myth we have about ourselves, then recovery might also be achieved by an act of will. To accomplish it, we need a myth that is even more compelling.

New York, it is said, has been living on the edge for years. It flirts with death; it plays Russian roulette, and no one can ever be sure that it will re-emerge after its next crisis. The most recent scare took place in the 1970s. During the years of the post-war boom, manufacturing industry moved out, to be replaced by office jobs, service industry, and – not so welcome – urban poverty and inner-city decline. Then, suddenly, the building industry collapsed. Office vacancies soared and new construction ceased. The new Second Avenue subway trench being dug south of Harlem had to be filled in. The essential services went on strike. The city panicked. Public funds were exhausted. Civic bankruptcy was in sight. And Washington refused to help.

And then, like characters in a John Buchan novel or a DC comic, New Yorkers rallied and with one bound were free from their fetters. They formed 'Save New York' groups, wore Big Apple badges, and covered their cars with the now ubiquitous and much imitated 'I Love NY' slogan, designed by Milton Glaser. And it worked – the city managed to talk itself out of trouble, pulling off the most extraordinary confidence trick of all time. Public services were trimmed, debts cleared, and the financial bandwagon made to roll again. And more – the city now sold itself to new markets. Corporations that had never thought they needed to be in New York in its healthiest days began to rush to its door. Foreign banks and insurance companies moved into Manhattan as a stepping stone to larger American markets. By the end of the 1970s, New York had overtaken London as the banking capital of the world.

That, at least, is the story which New Yorkers like to tell, and tell with an infectious enthusiasm. The reality is less attractive. It was not just a case of a community working together for the common good. There were real tragedies when companies went to the wall; careers were wrecked, commercial failures exploited. Cynically exploited, one might say, by biters driven by their fear of finding themselves the bitten. Everyone knew the rules, and there was little to tell between the vultures and the corpses they picked at. . . .

It is easy to fall for New York's rhetoric. Even when you know the facts, the story is just as dramatic, and just as clichéd, as the two-minute version. Without adopting the ideologies of the Eastern bloc, Manhattan manages to be its own censor. Without direct intervention or official menace, it controls the presentation of its public image. New Yorkers can tell you with disarming sincerity and simplicity that they just *love* their city. It does not take long before you are tuned into a mood of non-stop sensation which both deadens and hypnotises you into believing that New York is indeed the most important, the most dramatic, the most *crucial* city in the history of civilisation.

Then you look at the physical condition of New York: pot-holes in the roads, burned-out Harlem tenements, drug pushers on the sidewalks up in the 120s, the barricaded yellow cabs, graffiti-covered subway cars, graffiti-covered artists' canvases. A city pulsating with vigour? The most dynamic town in the world? Yes, if you have a myth that lets you interpret the city that way.

Down in Tribeca, a few sweat shops for the garment business still hang on in an area being overrun by photographic studios, art galleries, and restaurants – temples, all, to different kinds of self-gratification. For the Hoffman pressers next door or the truck drivers trying to unload outside, there is nothing in this that is flattering or comfortable. But they will tell you just as swiftly as the yuppies and frumpies that there is nowhere else like it, nowhere else they would rather be.

One of the nastiest places in New York is Hell's Kitchen, an area up in the mid-40s on 9th and 10th Avenues. Until about 1910, it had a reputation as the centre of Irish gang warfare and probably the most dangerous place in the whole of America. Since then, it has been colonised by Italians and after them, Puerto Ricans – an overlapping of cultures celebrated in *West Side Story*. Today, artists and actors are taking over from the sex shops, the dope peddlers, and the dispossessed blacks as the new ethnic minority. They are spending money rehabilitating old slum tenements and turning abandoned churches into theatres, which has not made Hell's Kitchen any prettier, but has given it the opportunity to express a new will to survive.

'I wouldn't want to live anywhere else but New York,' says one new Hell's Kitchen resident – a singer. 'The energy of the city, the cultural advantages of the city. . . . As a performer, it has everything that I need – all the music and theatre and dance. I don't know, just walking out of the door is an exhilarating experience.'

'We all know it's a tough city,' says a young Greek actor. 'I don't want to put a time limit on it but if I don't make it within, say, the next ten years I will most probably move out. Because New York is not for older people or people with no money. It's just for young people and people who made it. Otherwise, it's a very tough city.'

Mr Carnavelli who runs a delicatessen store on 9th Avenue is also philosophical. 'New York is a state of mind. It's supposed to be the place to be; it always was and probably always will be. The people who come over here just love New York. It's a great place to be.'

Three authentic voices of New York – each one a cliché in its own way, and important because of that, not in spite of it. Clichés are important for New York; they're the short-hand for what the city is held to represent. They are reminders that New York is not simply a place – or perhaps, not even a place – but the promise of a better future, the first staging post of the New World, the city that grew up behind Ellis Island, where a cliché is not just an over-worked expression but an immigrant's dream. Clichés have to be chanted like a litany, and they have to be believed. Behind them lie the irreconcilable realities of the Old World, whose problems could only be solved by escaping from them.

The same definition of the city's mythology is enshrined in its street pattern. Manhattan has a rational street plan – unlike the twisting, narrow, medieval streets that still characterise Europe. It is laid out like a grid, with twelve avenues running north to south, and 156 streets crossing them east to west. This gives it a most un-European quality: when you stand on a sidewalk and look into the distance, what you see is Nothing, just empty sky; the prospect is, as it were, open-ended. Unlike the streets of the Old World, the streets of New York do not lead from place to place; they lead from no place to no place. The only place to be is where one is. The streets promise the reality of a destination without ever delivering it. They also offer a way out. For an immigrant, that is enough.

The Manhattan Grid is both idealistic and pragmatic. The

brainchild of Gouverneur Morris, it was devised simply to make the control and acquisition of real estate easier at a time, in 1811, when the island was yet to be staked out and developed. By creating an inviolable network of roads, it was intended to prevent the corrupt European process by which the property of the public and the poor could be eroded by the accretions of the rich. It did not work, of course, or at least, it forced the wealthy to operate in new ways. But the immediate effect of the grid was to colonise the island of Manhattan conceptually, and it did so without needing to lay a single brick, and without making any concession to the lie of the land. It made Manhattan the first instant city and the first anti-city. It was a city without hierarchy or emphasis on any of the signs of natural life. It was from the start an invention of the human mind.

Like the American constitution, the grid guaranteed New Yorkers the freedom to pursue their own definitions of themselves within their private plots of land. It is an activity they still indulge in with obsessive relish. Talking clichés about New York is a civic pastime; the platitudes are so well worn that they have acquired the status of revelation, and a revelation that grows more revealing the more familiar it becomes. New York clichés confer on their users the title of amateur sociologist, for everyone except people like Richard Sennett of New York University; he is a professional.

'I don't think it's the dirt, the noise, the crime, the ills commonly ascribed to New York that are what really bothers other Americans about it,' says Sennett. 'It's the fact that it's a city in which people who are different have to live together. It's a city in which all the American myths about equality are shattered. Those myths of equality are really based on the notion of being equal with other people who are also like you.

'I think in the repertoire of experiences that people want to have in American cities, there's a profound contradiction. On the one hand, people do want to have an experience which transcends the intimate, the safe, the housed. On the other hand, they want to be intimate, safe, and housed, where they have no experience of difference. That's a contradiction which in New York has been kept up until fairly recently in a certain kind of balance. And now we're losing that balance. And part of the reason we're losing it is that planners really don't have a very good idea of how you create a space in which people feel exposed to each other but in which they also feel secure.'

Ada Louise Huxtable, who in 1970 won a Pulitzer Prize for her work as architecture critic on the *New York Times*, agrees that something is beginning to go seriously wrong. 'I'm a New Yorker, I grew up here, and I remember it very well twenty years ago. It's a city that is breaking down in terms of infrastructure. It's a city in which so much that is so exciting and so wonderful and so dramatic must be used as an excuse for things that are so very bad. You move around the city with much greater difficulty, traffic is worse, transportation is worse, the subway is infinitely worse. The conditions on the street are worse. It's harder to walk in New York, to take one elementary thing. It's a city in which you must be young and strong and responsive to a very special kind of financial and cultural stimulation to put up with what is really an insult to life.

'I feel very strongly about it, because I think it's unnecessary and improper, that it is the fault of a breakdown in planning, of greed within the real-estate community and within the city administration which is only interested in the tax base.[1] I am not a starry-eyed idealistic planner; I know that planning is an *ad hoc* and empirical process if it is going to work well, but I think you must have vision and structure in a city this size.'

Among the agents trying to juggle the need for vision against the suspicion it arouses and the belief in simple pragmatism are the city authorities and the property developers. In European cities, planning authorities have the upper hand, if simply by their power of veto; no one has an automatic right to build. In New York, the situation is different. All planning law is premised on the notion that a landowner has a constitutional right to develop his land – a right protected by law. The city authority can therefore only act as moderator, trying to create balance and to prevent excess. New York's City Planning Commission has zoning laws designed, for example, to limit buildings to heights that are appropriate to their surroundings, but such zoning is only a limitation of the pre-existing right to build. In addition, all legislation is negotiable, especially in the last ten years, when public funds have been scarce, because the City has not had enough money to carry out its own building programme. So to get anything built, it has invariably had to come in on the back of private schemes and trade generous planning concessions, that will certainly be to the advantage of the developer, for other features that it hopes will be to the advantage of the public – subway improvements, sidewalk repairs, and so on. And this is entirely to the liking of the developer because it invites him to enter negotiations about exceeding the

[1]New Yorkers pay city tax, as well as state and federal taxes.

available limits. It means that the entire thrust of a planning application in New York comes down to the question not of whether an applicant can build, but of how much he can build. The developer therefore has very much the upper hand.

One man who has hired his gun to both sides – planners and developers – is John Zuccotti. A former lawyer, he rose to become Deputy Mayor of New York and a Chairman of the City Planning Commission. Now he has gone back to the legal profession, helping to steer his clients in the estate business through the complicated web of planning legislation he had previously helped to enforce. It is a cleverly negotiated career, and one in which Mr Zuccotti has played sheriff and cowboy on a production quite as dramatic as any John Ford western.

'The real-estate business in the United States is probably the last frontier of the individual entrepreneur,' he says. 'It tends not to be bureaucratic, not to be institutionalised, but rather personalistic in the way it reflects an individual's ambition about how a property should be designed and put together and acquired. New York City is in fact a city that's been built on aggressive capitalism – no question about that – and on a tremendous material drive. And some of that is expressed in a desire to outdo X or outdo Y and build yet bigger buildings. I keep hearing stories that one or two of our developers are still hoping to build a building bigger than the World Trade Center.'

Such an ambition is, however, what the estate business in New York is all about. The religion of the city is the cult of individuality; buildings are its icons and developers are its priests. Among the most famous is Harry Helmsley, owner of seven Manhattan hotels, managing agent for many of the largest offices, and a high-ranking figure on the *Forbes 400* index to the wealthiest people in America. There is Sam Lefrak, who built a housing complex in Queens the size of a small suburb and called it Lefrak City. And there is young Donald Trump, who had the nerve to advertise his ambitious Trump Tower development on Fifth Avenue as 'the most exciting architectural experience of all time'. The substance for this claim amounted to a black-glass exterior, a pink-marble and brass interior, duplex and triplex apartments with views over Central Park, and two liveried black footmen on the doors. He also let it be known, erroneously as it turned out, that Prince Charles was going to be taking one of the apartments. Both Sam Lefrak and Donald Trump, not to mention Donald Trump's father, are on the *Forbes 400* too.

'It's a great game,' says Ada Louise Huxtable, 'and the

developers play it not only for maximum stakes but more than maximum stakes, so that they can afford to come down a little bit and act as if *they've* made the great concession. When someone like Donald Trump came up with a large building for the site of the Bonwit-Teller store on Fifth Avenue, the first thing he did was what every other developer does: show the critics, show the Planning Commission, show the press, models of the beautiful building they want to build and then the terrible building that they can build *as of right* under the City's laws, and which they *will* build unless the City gives them the variances and the exemptions so that they can build this perfectly beautiful building which breaks the laws of the city and gives them more than they're entitled to. And what the developer never says is that there is not a corporation in the country who will take space in those [tall, thin as-of-right buildings favoured by New York City regulations] because they've got to have larger floors than those needle floors thrusting up into the sky. The developer never says it, and no one else is knowledgeable enough to point it out. So there he is with an illegitimate negotiating tool which he uses right down to the ground.'

The world which such men inhabit is kept buoyant by its own extravagance. Excess is its baseline. George .Klein started out selling popcorn in Brooklyn. Today, he is head of the Park Tower Realty Corporation and one of the most stylish developers in Manhattan, with a reputation for going only to the elite of the architectural profession's commercial wing – I. M. Pei, Edward Larrabee Barnes, Philip Johnson. It is with Johnson that he recently won the coup of the decade – permission to redevelop Times Square, a scheme that will involve him in refurbishing the 42nd Street subway – the dirtiest and most dangerous subway station in Midtown. That is the gain to the city; the gain to the Park Tower Realty Corp is the permission to build up to 55 storeys without set-backs – which seems to flout the existing zoning laws without any compunction.

George Klein's own office is a two-storey penthouse which crowns the building he developed at 499 Park Avenue. Designed by I. M. Pei, the building has the geometrical elegance of a Braun cigarette lighter. Within its black-glazed façade, it contains an accumulation of corporate status symbols. The multi-storey foyer is paved in granite and decorated with the classic ornaments of such spaces – a huge wall painting, in this case by Dubuffet – and the ubiquitous fig tree, *Ficus benjamina*. The ultimate status symbol, however, is Mr Klein's office. You travel up 26 floors in an elevator to find the two floors of his suite connected by a private staircase. It is as if the final ascent to the boardroom has to be made on foot.

George Klein's definition of architectural quality is very simple. 'If you make curves instead of straight lines, it costs more money. If you cut slices out of buildings, that costs money.[1] Granite for the exterior of your building is much more expensive than concrete; quality glass is more money than cheap glass. The company that wants to project an image in its brochures will spend a great deal of money on designers for its stationery and use high quality paper for the letterhead of the president of the corporation or for their merchandising programmes. Therefore, when they are trying to make a statement, the building that they are in makes just as important a statement if not a more important statement.' Buildings are another branch of public relations.

The skyscraper is the epitome of self-promotion. It conforms to no architectural tradition. It knows no decorative rules. There is no aesthetic to say how high it should be or what it should look like. It is simply a steel skeleton for duplicating the site on which it is built, and it works by stacking potentially infinite reproductions of the ground one on top of another. Like redwoods in a forest of giant sequoias, the skyscraper's one ambition is to break the height barrier. In that sense, it is the very mascot of America – of self-expression, of unrestrained growth, of aspiration.

Not everyone revels in its poetic connotations, but New Yorkers are fatalistic. Pioneers don't have a track record of dealing with problems; they live with them until they get too big to handle, and then they move on. Arthur Drexler, Director of Architecture and Design at New York's Museum of Modern Art, has said in an exhibition on skyscrapers held in his department: 'While skyscrapers exploit land values to the point of rendering cities uninhabitable, there is no reason to stop building them since in a free society, Capitalism gives us what we want, including our own demise.'

Nor is it in the spirit of New York to prevent expansion, for developers are not a special privileged class, like traditional British landowners; they are the distillation of the ordinary man, the heroes of the masses. To restrain them is to restrain a basic instinct shared by the entire community – even though, as Arthur Drexler suggests, it may be the instinct of lemmings. To curb the developer would be just as much an affront to freedom as the licensing of guns.

[1]This is in fact a device for circumventing height restrictions by satisfying planning limitations concerned with the penetration of daylight to the street. It is therefore by no means a liability to the developer.

This does not mean it has never been tried. On the contrary, it is always being tried; it never works, because the perpetual struggle to contain the excesses of development are always offset by an enthusiasm for the benefits it might bring. This paradox, which prevents the City planners from exercising any real muscle, goes back 170 years to Manhattan's early days. The city authorities effectively wrote themselves out of the game right from the start by laying down ground rules which – they failed to anticipate – would put themselves at a disadvantage. Gouverneur Morris's gridiron matrix ensured that the first planners to have a decisive influence on New York City would also be the last. The gridiron did not just fix the format of the city; it also circumscribed the possibility of future municipal invention. Instead of trimming the sails of private builders, Morris had trimmed his own sails. The new street plan made it possible for him to predict exactly *where* the city would grow but it left wide open *how* it would grow. All responsibility for that was from then on consigned to private hands.

The flood gates had been unleashed, but the flood did not come at once. It was not until the late nineteenth century, when the port of New York finally took over from Boston, Charleston and the older ports on the Eastern seaboard as the main gateway to America, that commercial institutions began to flock to Lower Manhattan. The competition for space and prestige was reflected in a reckless race for buildings that would outdo their neighbours – a race that culminated in 1915 in the construction by the Equitable Insurance Company of a 41-storey skyscraper on Lower Broadway. The building put its rivals in the shade – as it was meant to – rather too literally; it cast a seven-acre shadow across them, stealing their light, and threatening to undermine their real-estate value. It was only then, when architecture began to upset rather than enhance the financial stability of the community, that the City was pressured into acting. It did what no other American city had done: it introduced planning controls.

The following year, in 1916, a zoning resolution was adopted which aimed at pleasing all interested parties. It would try to satisfy those building owners whose properties were at risk, without doing anything to prejudice further developments. The intention was to regulate the design of new towers so that sunlight might still penetrate through to the street. Rather perversely, it took as its model the Woolworth Building, which by then had overtaken the Equitable to become, at 60 storeys, the tallest building in the world. This now became the pattern for future development, for what the new law effectively did was to legalise retroactively everything that had been built up to that date.

The way the law operated was an ingenious blurring of a visual concept and an abstract procedure – the traditional balancing act of New York. It talked in terms of envelopes of space. Above every city *block* – the rectangles of land contained between intersecting streets – it specified a given volume of air within which building could take place. New buildings were allowed to occupy the entire area of the block up to a specified height, usually based on the width of the street which the block fronted. Above this height, the façade of the building had to be set back. But the centre 25 per cent of the land could contain a tower of unlimited height.

The principle behind this regulation was that since each block was invariably sub-divided into very much smaller parcels of land, it could not be over-built. What was not forecast was that companies would buy up these smaller sites in order to acquire entire blocks, which would in turn enable them to get the bonus of an unrestricted central tower. The effect was that, instead of putting a check on New York's growth, there now took place the biggest building boom in the city's history, and one characterised by the stepped 'wedding cake' skyscrapers of the 1920s and early '30s, the most extravagant of which – the Empire State Building – was nevertheless, at 102 storeys, a faithful interpretation of the new law.

Building went into decline during the Depression and only recovered after the war, when it was aided by the new and cheaper buildings techniques introduced by immigrant architects from Nazi Europe. Among them was the German architect Ludwig Mies van der Rohe, who had briefly run the Bauhaus School in its last years, up until its closure in 1933. On his arrival in America, he became head of the Chicago School of Architecture at the University of Illinois and continued to work in the style he had developed in the 1920s – open-plan, severely rectangular buildings in which all the structural load was carried on steel or steel-clad columns that allowed the walls to dematerialise into sheets of glass.

In 1954, Mies won the commission to build a New York office for Seagram, the Canadian-based firm of whisky distillers.[1] Mies' solution was quite unprecedented by real-estate standards. Instead of building to the very edges of the site, he set the building back from the line of its neighbours. His argument was aesthetic. Zoning limitations specified a maximum square footage, and

---

[1] See page 85 for an account of the events which led to this.

spreading this maximum over the whole area of the site would produce a building that was fat and dumpy. But by giving up part of the site, he could concentrate the building over a smaller area and produce a building that at 37 storeys was taller and more elegant, with, at its base, an outdoor courtyard with a pair of fountains.

The Seagram Building came as a revelation to architects. In fact it was nothing more than a 25 per cent tower without a base, but it had the effect of delivering a streamlined snub at all the architects who, until then, had religiously interpreted zoning laws in terms of squat profiles, fussy ledges, and stale ornamentation. It also demonstrated a new approach to building, a new use of materials, and a new relationship to the street. The courtyard, or plaza, was immediately taken up by an enthusiastic public, who began to use it as a rendezvous spot, somewhere to sit out in the sun at lunchtime, to read the papers and eat their sandwiches.

Within a few years, so many new offices were going up, especially on the traditionally residential Park and Madison Avenues, that a public outcry arose. It was felt that zoning had become too complicated and too open-ended for the planners to administer effectively. There were horror stories about New York becoming over-built, and a general appeal for reform. Once again, the City had to act, but not in so draconian a way as to harm the interests of the forces it was trying to curtail. Their solution, made possible by the Seagram Building, emerged in 1961, the year following the outcry of 1960.

William H. Whyte, author of *The Organisation Man* and a professional observer of the city, contributed to a 1969 policy document on the future of New York. Several of his observations were based on his experience of previous attempts at legislation. 'One of the effects of the 1961 zoning was to down-zone and say: "Builders, you cannot go as high as you used to." Now this was a little bit of a gambit because the City then turned round and said: "However, we will let you go back up higher if you give us something in return – specifically, give us a Seagram's plaza." They didn't actually say a Seagram's plaza but it's interesting, if you go back to the actual wording, it in effect asks for a Seagram's plaza. That was in 1961, and I remember writing about it with great pride in the 1969 plan for New York – we bragged: "Isn't this wonderful!" Since that time, every new office building in New York incorporated the plaza bonus and we got something like 28 acres more open space created by New York City than in all the other cities in the country combined.

'Then it began to dawn on us that nobody was using these plazas. They were dead. Not Seagram's – Seagram's was a wonderful place – but with most of the other plazas, all the developer did was to put some empty space there. There was no place to sit; often if there was a ledge it would have spikes on it so you couldn't sit on the thing. The City was being had.'

In 1975, zoning laws were changed again in an attempt to win a few civic amenities from the massively profitable private schemes that were taking place. Just as the Seagram Building had been the model for one sort of bonus, the outdoor courtyard, so a new building – the Citicorp Building – became the model for another – the indoor courtyard, or atrium. The Citicorp atrium was enormously popular; as well as providing a covered route from one side of the block to the other, it also contained restaurants, cafés, and shops, including Conran's – the New York version of Terence Conran's furniture chain which trades in Britain as Habitat – all disposed in a loose, open-plan version of the European shopping arcade or mall. Citicorp was all the good things of life, under cover. From then on, New Yorkers needed never to see daylight again.

Like the stepped skyscraper and the plaza, the atrium quickly became established as the cliché of the late 1970s, and was as quickly exploited. Where the plaza had been a gift to the public, the atrium, with its waterfalls and pools and Japanese gardens and granite floors and air-conditioning and shops and eateries, was a gift to the developer. It introduced a new tier of commercial activity into the building by attracting pedestrians to spend casual money in its attractive, idealised environment. And still the developers got their extra storeys and other concessions from the planners – as if they had suffered a loss that needed compensating for. Once again, the planning authority was helping to stimulate the very thing it was trying to avoid.

Two explanations for this persistent failure of the authorities suggest themselves. The first is a memory of the way the Wall Street crash had sent American investment into a state of shock. Struck by this, New York's financial psychologists recommended a course of aversion therapy when crisis loomed in the 1970s. The moment the patient regained consciousness, they told him to get up and start building again. And it worked. Having suffered a breakdown only five or six years earlier, the real-estate community in New York soon became neurotically confident. In 1982, Manhattan saw 7.5 million square feet of new office space completed, which is more than was built in the previous six years put together; and all of it was spoken for within the year. 1983 added a further 17 office buildings, taking the two-year total of additional lettable space to nearly 20 million square feet. If a business community can talk its way out of trouble, then this scale of investment speaks volumes: about 200 million cubic feet, in fact.

The fascination with extravagance as a commodity of survival is illustrated in the sales pitch that George Klein gives out. 'I think that New York is probably the single most dynamic market in the United States and maybe in the world. It has the largest [commercial] square footage of any city in the world. There is more square footage in New York than Los Angeles, Chicago, Washington, Boston and Houston combined. It is the world centre of finance, the world centre of commerce, an extremely diverse and probably the most fascinating real-estate city in the world. New York has shown enormous flexibility of growth. There is no such thing as an inexhaustible supply. However, the foreseeable future shows that there is great need still for additional space in New York, and the fascinating part of it is that there is a real-estate recession in the United States today. The only city that has held up, both in the sense of rentals and in the sense of tenants, is New York City.'

A second explanation for municipal impotence is the city's attitude to the quality of life. According to the Dutch architect and polemicist Rem Koolhaas, Manhattan's success contains the spectre of its possible failure. But he adds: 'Manhattan is an accumulation of possible disasters that never happen.' The disasters never happen because the definition of disaster keeps changing. The city keeps asking its citizens whether they can accommodate themselves to the new excesses and the reply is always, yes. One person who, inadvertently perhaps, has helped to redefine New York's definitions and made palatable the affronts that Ada Louise Huxtable points to is William Whyte. His studies of street life have shown that people can accommodate themselves as happily as cockroaches to the conditions they find themselves in.

'One of the first things we noticed when we were doing our studies of street life', says Whyte, 'was what happens when two friends run into each other, and I was very interested to find out how far out of the pedestrian traffic stream they would move. And I hypothesised that they would move right next to a building [into that strip of sidewalk] that people never use. So we mounted time-lapse cameras and we saw quite the contrary. People didn't move out of the traffic stream; they moved *into* it. And the longer the conversation, the more apt they were to be in the middle.

'If you ask those people what kind of sitting space they would like, they tell you "Oh, I want quiet, a walled enclave, a lot of greenery, somewhere to get away from the city." In fact, they never go near such a place. For example, Greenacre Park on 53rd Street is very small – it's all of 42 feet by 100 feet – and it's very simple and people will tell you how quiet and uncrowded it is. It is in fact the most crowded place of its kind in New York. It is quite noisy. The decibel count is quite high. On a nice summer day, the place will be jammed with about 180 people, which is a lot for a small place. Yet they don't feel crowded. They have little rituals of moving their chairs just a fraction from the next person, as if to say: "It's all right, I don't want to encroach on your space." And then they can eat their sandwiches or read a book and not feel cramped.

'It's wonderful to see how people can enjoy a rather high density as long as they feel there's a choice. So when I go to other cities and I don't see much of that, I feel a little proud of New York. The reason I don't see it in other cities is that there is simply not enough density of people. It's like a party – you need a certain number of people to make the thing work. And this is the mark of a great city.'

William Whyte's is a very different interpretation from that of Richard Sennett who, in his book *The Fall of Public Man*, has talked about the paradox of people being isolated by their own visibility in the open-plan offices, the glass walls, and the dead public space of the modern city. In Dr Sennett's world, threat is always present; Mr Whyte's New York seems to be a safer, more sociable place in which isolation is a matter of choice, while chance meetings are virtually unavoidable.

'People love to talk about the anonymity of a great city. But you often find more human contact in a very crowded place than in a less crowded place. We have, for example, quite a few street characters, and one of the greatest contributions they make is what I call *triangulation*. What I mean by that is that they furnish a connection between people that otherwise doesn't exist. For example, you and I are standing on a street corner, and we don't know each other from Adam. Mr Magoo is our traffic director. He's a wonderful character and he's a typical New Yorker – he's got a rasping voice, very brusque, very rude, and he's out there directing traffic and calling things like: "Hey, lady, where the hell d'ya think you're goin'?" And people are there and they're laughing. And I turn to you and say: "Do you know who that guy is?" and I'll say it in a tone of voice you reserve for close friends. And you'll say: "I saw him the other week," or "I think he's a cop," or something like that. You will go away, but for one brief instance, we talked.'

When William Whyte was asked to work with the City Planning Commission in compiling the City's 1969 policy document, he responded by avoiding making any impositions on developers – for which they must surely have been grateful. Instead, he tried simply to express the genius of the city, and to do so at a time when decentralisation was in vogue. The dominant issue in the Manhattan volume of the plan – the part that attracted most attention – was the statement that a certain amount of congestion was actually valuable. Jonathan Barnett, a writer on urban design and professor of architecture and urban design at New York's City College, was particularly impressed by Mr Whyte's impact on the plan.

'Congestion was another name for the kind of contact that made cities effective,' he says, 'and that was Holly Whyte's contribution. Had the text been only by planners it would have said something like: "Under certain circumstances, it is conceivable that an increased density in certain types of central commercial land uses is advantageous." No one would have paid any attention to that, but Holly Whyte said "Congestion can be good"' – a quip which might equally have applied to plumbers and bronchial specialists. But it was the property developers – once again, those with most to gain – who must have been most grateful for this impartial endorsement; it made their most self-serving business activities seem like acts of civic benevolence. If the Real Estate Board of New York Inc. had gone to Madison Avenue for a public relations campaign, they could hardly have been better served.

Congestion is usually the thing that planning tries to alleviate. To argue that it was desirable and worth preserving flew in the face not just of all conventional theory – conventional for the late 1960s, that is – but also the limited techniques by which planners operate. Planning aims to make things simpler, to separate conflicts of function, and where possible to clear the ground for new, more rational uses.

'The blank canvas approach was very heady stuff for architects and developers who generally do their worst work when they're allowed their full scope,' says Mr Whyte, 'and that's when you see these massive towers and very little attention to pedestrian scale. You know, an individual big building is one thing, but when you get colonies of them, it changes their character.

'One of the best things about some of our new developments is the fact that there isn't too much of it, or to put it another way, it's the old tacky stuff around it [that saves it]. Take Third Avenue. It's being redeveloped now but it still has some wonderful tacky blocks and these are very functional. Not just because down in the basement of one of those little brownstones there's a liquor store or a dry-cleaner's – the kind of stores you simply don't see in the great big structures. There's something else: they've got scale. For instance, take a look at the Citicorp Building. The Citicorp Building is not suburban, you know you're in the city, but one of the reasons you know you're in the city is not because of the Citicorp Building itself but its surroundings. Now, if you tear down the surroundings, as is actually happening, and put up Son of Citicorp, then you change something. I think the worst thing that can happen to the Citicorp Building is to have Son of Citicorp, but I'm afraid that's what we're going to get.'

Whether William Whyte is able to protect the shoddy side of New York depends on which of two views of the city prevails. His vision of congestion and tackiness as creative abuses may have given the Planning Commission a certain leeway to indulge the worst excesses of the estate community, but his brand of optimism about what New York represents is a new and challenging – or it would be better to say, old and challenging – phenomenon that threatens to undermine the very genius of New York that he has tried to identify in his theoretical work.

In New York, hype is hope. It is not so much a dishonest or a cynical activity as a naïve expression of a faith in a future whose potential is always more attractive than the actuality of the present. Television news shows and chat shows, for example, rely on trails of up-and-coming items in order to keep their audience. Trails promise an excitement and a potential which are always yet to be fulfilled and therefore yet to disappoint; they divert attention away from the material actually being broadcast, because such material always fails to live up to the claims made for it. The reality of TV news shows is so much the opposite of the potential they wish to embody that their only role is to be constantly disposed of or abandoned. Where British television flatters all its programmes by the courtesy of polite continuity, television in New York is a fragmented succession of interruptions, abbreviations, and abrupt edits. The outcome is a product which fails to satisfy because it lacks respectful treatment, and lacks respectful treatment because it fails to satisfy.

The same applies to New York's buildings. Behind the plush façades and marble foyers which serve as come-ons to the prospective shopper or business client or hotel guest, the sophistication breaks down. Those parts of the building meant to be out of bounds to the public, or which only get visited by service staff – fire escapes, service corridors, rear entrances and delivery points – are often quite remarkably crude. Not just unadorned, but so horribly cheap in their construction, in the clumsy threading of essential cables and plumbing, in the unintended uses they are put to (notably, temporary storage), and their general state of upkeep, that it is amazing that they go on working, that the supply of mains water still reaches the topmost floors, or that the worn electric wiring does not short across the metal down-pipes.

This is the reality that lies behind the façade, made possible by its relationship with the façade. To lure more shoppers and clients and guests, New York buildings do what television does, and trail on their exteriors the coming attractions of their interiors. To do this, they pinch pennies from the utilitarian parts of the building, since these represent reality and reality is, if not expendable, then at least too mundane to be worth consideration. This automatically rules out the possibility of *all* parts of a building being treated with equal care.

Such glorification of the cosmetic is a challenge to all previous notions of where the limits of unacceptability lie. By stressing the compensations of living in a certain way, the overall deterioration is made to seem not just tolerable but challenging and dramatic. Every summit of civic abuse becomes the plateau for a new abuse. As a private consultant, William Whyte was able to suggest to the City Planning Commission the engaging notion that congestion could be good. But he did so not because he was in the business of urban cosmetics but for the opposite reason – because of a faith in the homespun. William Whyte's arguments in favour of New York as it was were a reflection not of youthful, thrusting ambition but a more mature contentment, a willingness to abide with the familiar, even a lack of vision. Home Sweet Home. All's well with the world.

But that was in 1969. In 1982, the Planning Commission looked around at the results of that policy and decided that, on the contrary, all was not well with the world, especially not that part of the world most in demand with developers – the thirty blocks south of Central Park, between 30th and 59th Streets, and between Second and Eighth Avenues.

'There was a public perception that things had gotten pretty bad,' remarks the Chairman of the Commission, Herbert Sturz. 'Canyons were starting to become visible in Midtown and we spent a lot of effort dealing with the Community Boards, with many enlightened developers, and with the elected officials. And really, they all came to believe that you could kill the so-called golden egg of Midtown Manhattan on the East Side, that it could get so hot in that area for development that it would become counter-productive. Particularly, we were concerned with sky-scrapers being shoe-horned into all the mid-blocks. We believed that if nothing was done about this, you would start seeing the old six-storey buildings being taken down and replaced with 50-storey buildings, so that not only would you have the canyon effect on the avenues but on the mid-blocks as well. That would have been a disaster for New York.'

Herbert Sturz's response was to try to down-zone Midtown, thereby preventing developers from building as high and as intensively as they had been doing. Observers said it could not be done – that the estate lobby was too strong, that their rights were too heavily protected in law, and that in any case too many members of the City Council had vested interests in property to allow the new legislation to go through. In fact, the Commission won, though their victory may have amounted to nothing more than delaying tactics. Their reason for intervening, as Mr Sturz pointed out, was a fear not so much that the quality of life might be damaged but that estate prices might be harmed *if* the quality of life was damaged. This is what the Commission had to convince the developers of.

The crux of the debate was to get across the idea that there were limits: limits to the inconveniences that commercial tenants would put up with for the sake of having a Manhattan address; limits to the overcrowding that transport users and pedestrians would put up with on the streets, the sidewalks, and the subways; limits to how long assaults could be made on the appearance of the city. The problem lay in finding evidence to back this message up. In theory, perhaps, tenants and public might object to the quality of life; in fact, the city went on functioning. To protect a particular image of urban life was to protect an image which had outraged a previous generation; it was to institutionalise processes of commercialism which in their own time had also been exploitative. Where was the logic in that? New York's image had changed so much in recent years, and was still changing, that to talk about an acceptable status quo was meaningless. Previous disasters had turned out not to be disasters; why should this one be?

By the same token, nothing in the city deserved protection, because everything old was an invitation to stagnation and an obstacle to something better. During the post-war boom, the concept of conservation hardly existed. Anything already built was fair game, as long as the economics worked out. So the city stood by and watched as a trail of demolition took place.

But as brownstones, walk-ups, and even modest little 14-storey offices were bulldozed, public concern did mount. The straw that broke the camel's back was the destruction in 1963 of Pennsylvania Station – with its Italianate hall in the style of the Baths of Caracalla, designed by McKim, Mead and White between 1906–10. This time, there was uproar and to quell disquiet, the City grudgingly agreed to intervene. It was rather like the morning after the blight before; and besides, their action was two years coming.

When it came, however, a declaration was made that some buildings should be officially protected as landmarks, and prevented from being developed. But since many of them had been bought with the intention of future development, this legislation wiped out their commercial value. Now it was the developers who were up in arms, and the City was pressed into compensating them for their hypothetical loss by inventing a new tier of property ownership which gave a commercial value to thin air. They decreed that the envelope of developable air above every plot of land need no longer be attached to that plot but, like a dirigible, could be sold and hooked up to other sites. This is how the Philip Morris Corporation came to acquire the air rights of Grand Central Station for $2.2 million, enabling them to add an extra 74,655 square feet to the building they were putting up across the street.

That was not the only way in which this particular piece of protective legislation was turned upside down. By the side of many old churches in Midtown or Lower Manhattan, one can now find a skyscraper looming far higher than would previously have been allowed, thereby wrecking the aesthetic impact of the very building the law had meant to protect. In time, it may not even stand to one side; it may simply piggy-back on top of the landmark in order to get at its unused air.

How does Herbert Sturz of the Planning Commission account for this? 'We care about light and air,' he says, 'but we also know the city needs to grow. We want, if possible, to have it grow in areas that can best take it. There's an awareness that in some cases like 42nd Street and Times Square [George Klein's development], new uses can overwhelm old uses and good uses can overwhelm bad uses. This is better than simply trying to enforce something on the street. Enforcement hasn't worked.'

In other words, the power of the City authorities only comes into play when there is building going on; if there is no building, they have nothing to exercise power over. So they have to allow building to go ahead in order to give themselves the slightest chance of modifying it in its details. 'All zoning,' as Herbert Sturz's legal adviser Norman Marcus points out, 'gains its clout in areas of high land values. There are many areas of the city where zoning doesn't matter a damn' – because no one wants to build there.

This is aggravated by the fact that building costs are the same wherever one builds, so there is very little incentive to build in areas where the rentals returns will be low. This does not just mean Harlem and the South Bronx – it also means respectable but neglected parts of the city like West Midtown. So that, while the City can muscle in on schemes in areas where there is little need for intervention, they are impotent to help those areas where no building is going on.

The logic of New York is that everyone enjoys freedom from municipal intrusion, including those who need that intrusion most. When the City does step in, it is invariably those who need it least who gain – as happened in the down-zoning of Midtown, which only served to raise property values even higher by curbing growth.

It is often the case in New York that public functions are carried out by private individuals or corporations. With the squeeze on public funds, this process may now be starting to encroach on planning as well. Just as the failure of policing has led to residents' committees dealing in their own way with security matters, and to self-styled vigilante groups and 'guardian angels' taking the law into their own hands on the subways, so each district of Manhattan now has its own Community Board, staffed by volunteers who feel inadequately protected by the planning authority. Their role is recognised by the Planning Commission, and all planning applications have to be submitted to them for consideration, though their views do not need to be acted on. This trend points, nevertheless, to a call for moderation within the community – an attempt to discover, by consent, exactly where New York's limits lie.

The groups go for their advice to experts like Jonathan Barnett, although Dr Barnett is by no means a disinterested specialist; he is liable to work as urban design consultant for firms whose schemes the Community Boards might be deliberating on. It is that ambiguity in his own position which makes him of value to both residents and developers, and enables him to handle those issues which make planning a grey area rather than a matter of black and white.

'To some extent, the planning officials were dazzled by the famous architects and permitted buildings that were bigger than was strictly necessary,' says Barnett. 'IBM by Edward Barnes is a building which breaks certain of the basic "sky exposure plane" regulations. Philip Johnson's AT&T[1] which is just to the south of it has a floor area of 55 per cent of the site instead of 40 per cent. I. M. Pei and Partners' 499 Park Avenue has a 92 per cent floor and then the Philip Morris Building by Ulrich Franzen has 100 per cent coverage. The effect of these larger coverages is that they make the site developable for big buildings which could never have been developed without these special permissions. This means that the production of a high-quality building becomes an essential first step if the developer wants to get permission to build a building at all. So you have what I call the Trojan Horse syndrome: you get good architecture but you also have larger buildings.

'Of course the question is: how much is too much? That is: how much development makes a city intolerable? And your received wisdom on that in London is that the Barbican[2] is as dense as any development should be, and my recollection is that the Barbican is about 135 households per acre. We, in our highest residential density in New York, allow about two and a half times that – almost 300 apartments per acre.

'Now, what is the effect of that on the life of the community? I'm afraid no one really knows. Unfortunately, our development regulations are founded on a principle of accepting something that seemed acceptable and then saying "Well, maybe we can have a little more." It's like crossing a pond and not knowing whether the ice will break. If everyone were to flush a toilet in every building in Manhattan at the same time, which is a statistical possibility, what would the effect be on the sewage system? No one knows.

'What happens in American cities in particular is that development regulations have permitted a city which is three or four times as dense as anyone expects to be built. This is to allow competitive real-estate investment to take place and for developers to secretly assemble their plots and compete with each other. When the 1962 Zoning was passed everyone said that it brought the city down

---

[1]See pp. 94–6.
[2]A commercial development of leasehold flats built by the City of London.

from a potential city of 55 million people to a potential city of 13 million people. It is of course 7 million people at the present time. So that would mean that we are zoned for almost twice as dense a city as we are at present. And that's because of competition.'

The leeway that the City allows for development and the question of degree over what constitutes acceptable congestion are just two of the issues which make planning an imprecise science. To that extent, Jonathan Barnett extends the scope of the moral debate but does not contribute to its solution. For a solution, there has to be a showdown between deeply held convictions – between, for example, John Zuccotti and his favourite adversary Ruth Messinger, who serves as a City Councillor with a responsibility for 212,000 souls in West Manhattan, and sees it as her job to find some way to break through the potentially suicidal logic of New York.

'My concern has been that on the one hand, the City is not doing enough to intervene in the pattern of private development which is helping to squeeze out manufacturing industry from what is still the largest industrial city in the United States, and on the other hand that the City is in fact subsidising private development through a variety of overly-generous and mis-targeted tax benefit programmes,' she says. 'We are paying out about $200 million a year, by virtue of not collecting a property tax which ought to be paying for city services. And that subsidy is being obtained by a great many of Mr Zuccotti's clients – developers who are producing housing only for the wealthiest 2 or 3 per cent of the people who live in New York.'

'It is true that we are only developing housing at the upper-middle or luxury end of the scale,' Mr Zuccotti admits, 'but not through any problem with the developer. Developers would do subsidised housing as well as luxury housing if there were any subsidies. The problem is that there are no subsidies any longer. What we need to develop is some political consensus which says that these subsidy programmes that used to be the mainstay of balanced development have to be reintroduced.

'The other side of the story is that whether one likes it or not, growth and change are required for the city to continue to have some kind of economic viability. To the extent that we build new buildings, we increase the amount of rateables and therefore more revenue falls into the coffers of the City of New York. Which is why this conflict isn't just a conflict between public sector regulation and private sector development. It can be a conflict within the government itself, because the Planning Commission says "We want maximisation of light and air, maximisation of amenities, maximisation of urban design" ' and the Tax Commissioner says "I need to increase the revenue base of the City so we can balance our books." The very same debate is going on within the government itself.

'You see, the problem is this. Let's take a typical stockbrokerage firm. The senior people, the decision makers, obviously have to have face-to-face contact with their clients or with other peers in their business. But that doesn't mean the computer analyst has to, or the draughtsman has to, or the telephone operators have to. These back-office functions can be located in less expensive structures with lower rents, and the problem is that less expensive structures with lower rents do not exist on Manhattan Island, for the most part, and very often not in the city of New York. And given the nature of modern communications, it's possible to locate your computer centre, if you're a bank, in North Dakota and keep your main banking offices on Wall Street.'

Ruth Messinger is not impressed. 'There's an acronym that we use here that says the economy of New York City is based on FIRE, F-I-R-E, which stands for Finance, Insurance, and Real Estate. Those are the sectors of our economy that are growing and I believe that the City ought to recognise that each of those areas has a natural and compelling interest in New York and would continue to stay here and could very well support our service needs to a much greater extent than they do. Unfortunately, the City looks at it the other way round and in my judgement overly believes the real-estate community and its legal representatives like Mr Zuccotti when they say "Look, times were hard here once before, some people are thinking of leaving, maybe people would rather live in New Jersey, we'll only stay here if you assist," and assist means keeping these tax abatement programmes untouched and approving a variety of requests for changes in zoning.'

One of the mottoes of the City Planning Commission is a quotation from Heraclitus: 'Nothing endures but change' – an ironic acknowledgement, it would seem, of its own defeat. Manufacturing industry in New York is declining, and corporate industry is pulling out. On the other hand, in doing so they are leaving behind a ghost of themselves more physical than what had been there before. Industrial locations are more heavily used now than they were twenty years ago, while many of the companies that left in the 1960s and 1970s now have a larger number of employees in Manhattan than they had when they were officially based there. The threat of leaving New York City is both a business gambit and a reality. Both sides are right.

That people like Ruth Messinger and Ada Louise Huxtable are anxious about over-development shows that in spite of New York's reputation for aggressive capitalism, there are voices prepared to speak out on behalf of the community, and against the inhumanity of vested interests. But that is only part of the story. We invent cities; they then invent us, to the extent that the genius of New York as a place of ruthless expansion becomes an accepted – even a desired – interpretation not just among those doing the expanding but among those on the receiving end. As William Whyte has said,[1] the remarkable thing is the consensus of behaviour among New Yorkers, considering how many are newcomers. 'They come from all over, some from abroad, and for many the nearest thing to a downtown they've experienced before arriving is a suburban shopping mall. Acclimation is harsh, and quick. Soon they are walking fast. . . . They even come to appreciate the tawdriness and inconveniences and danger, reflecting as they do on the heroism of simply coping with New York. Above all, they are fascinated. They are at the center of the universe.'

To live comfortably, then, may not be the only virtue a city can provide; there may be other equally valuable forms of urban life. New York is not a machine for living, as Le Corbusier said of the house; it is a machine for doing business in – a magnificent catastrophe. And while the urge to prevent the quality of life from getting worse is admirable, it intrinsically threatens New York's ability to keep remaking itself and, in the nature of capitalism – and cancer – to sacrifice itself to the point of suicide in order simply to keep growing. And when New York stops growing, it is finished. It becomes a city tamed by civility.

Americans on the West Coast believe that this is already happening. They see New York as an irrelevance in terms of high-tech industry. Culturally too, they regard it as a transatlantic backwater of European conservatism. Californians were the immigrants who kept moving, the young men who continued going west until they found their final destination in the seaboard of the setting sun. For them, the open-ended streets of New York were only a transit station, not a place to stop. Those who stayed there lacked the energy for the real American adventure. Where the spirit that made New York has been prevented from expanding further, it has made its home in the west, or been suppressed.

A before-and-after example of New York's change of heart can

[1]*The WPA Guide to New York*, 1982 edition, Pantheon Books.

be seen in a planning scheme conceived in the 1960s by the then state governor Nelson Rockefeller. It was in the finest traditions of New York consumerism: rather than refurbish those residential districts that were in decay, he developed a plan to extend the waterfont on Manhattan's lower west side by creating 92 virgin acres. The site was to be transformed into a huge architectural juggernaut with residential tower blocks for about 28,000 residents – slightly more than the existing population of Lower Manhattan and about the same size as Monaco. It was also to contain separately zoned office blocks, ground-level highways, and pedestrian bridges that took no account of the Big Apple's traditional gridiron character.

Then came the crash of the 1970s, and Battery Park City, as it was known, was shelved – until 1979, when the City brought in Cooper Eckstut, a firm of private consultants, to try and salvage it. Cooper Eckstut found Rockefeller's vision impractical. They therefore abandoned the megastructure and the two levels of circulation for traffic and pedestrians, and instituted a street-and-block plan so typical of Manhattan that it even specified mandatory cornices at set heights on the new street façades.

This unprecedented nostalgia for the old – unprecedented for New York – has acted in other ways to depress new thinking. In 1983, developers were bidding to knock down the Lever Building, built in 1951 and the city's first example of a curtain-wall building. It was known that the glass walls needed complete replacement, and the cost of this combined with the building's only partial use of its site made redevelopment an attractive commercial proposition. Six years earlier in 1977, the owners of the Chrysler Building, one of the city's best-loved symbols, were also applying for demolition. At one time, New Yorkers might have looked forward to the buildings that were going to replace them, just as they looked forward to the completion of the Empire State Building on the site of the old Waldorf-Astoria. Instead, the Chrysler Building was restored and the Lever Building was designated a landmark in respect of its importance to architectural historians.

The significance of these and other cases is that they show New York becoming set in its ways, becoming satisfied with the image it has of itself. A similar situation is occurring among New York's residential population. Following the lead of artists who, in the absence of any other suitable studio accommodation, colonised the turn-of-the-century warehouses of SoHo and Tribeca, half the city now seems to regard the warehouse as the *sine qua non* of a

New York lifestyle.[1] Gentrification of Hell's Kitchen is already in full swing, and the same is reportedly about to happen in Harlem and the South Bronx, which seems incredible to anyone who knows their present distressed condition.

The movement of young urban professionals into previously no-go areas is explained by the rising cost of property in more fashionable districts – a syndrome which forces innocent home-makers into becoming shrewd property speculators in their own right. They in turn introduce into the real estate community the idea that there is now a market for older buildings in a way there was not before. But the syndrome is fuelled by a need – which was also not there before – to belong to a place with a sense of its own past. Old warehouses, abandoned tenements, disused churches, satisfy that need, which gives them a new scarcity value. But that sense of the past can also be manufactured, as it is being in the reapplication of old-fashioned building types at Battery Park City.

The impact of this conservatism is critical for New York. It is no longer the place it once was, precisely because it so much wants to be the place it once was. It is becoming middle-aged, attempting to recapture its youth by reverting to how it was in its youth, forgetting that it never reverted in such a way when it was younger. In its obsession with past achievements, it has jeopardised its sense of how it felt to be a city on the make. New Yorkers are still on the look-out for change, but change has become a ritual of consolation that operates at the very lowest level – new films, new fashions, new clubs, new restaurants – hardly anything that requires a complete emotional overhaul. It really is a case of *plus ça change*. If you really want change, you have to look to Los Angeles and the cities of the Pacific rim. New York is getting comfortable with itself, its anxieties, its inequities. It is finding itself.

But in finding itself, it is losing itself. All transactions have their price, and the price of domesticity is the loss of freedom. The artefacts that were once expendable are now the milestones of New York's future stagnation. In finding value in its own past, it has forfeited its ability to confront the future. Welcome to Europe, New York.

[1]See Tom Wolfe's comments, p. 135 *et seq.*

The Best Hated Architect in the World

When the American telecommunications giant AT&T went looking for an architect for their new corporate headquarters on New York's Madison Avenue in 1975, the man they went to was Philip Johnson. What they were asking for was a ticklish piece of architectural juggling. Like all American business empires, they wanted a building that would flatter their commercial ego, and enhance their 'name recognition', as the advertising industry puts it. They reckoned that for a modest outlay of $110 million, they could put up a building capable of being acclaimed 'the world's greatest skyscraper for the world's greatest corporation', and still have change in their pockets from their assets of $145 thousand million. At the same time, they wanted a design that was conservative enough to play down their public image; an anti-trust suit had been filed against them which could result (and in fact has done so) in AT&T's being dismantled and restructured.

What Philip Johnson gave them for their money was 13,000 tons of pink granite in the shape of an elongated Rolls Royce radiator, topped with a broken Roman pediment – a gesture so outlandish that it created waves of controversy and led to the building's being dubbed 'the Chippendale skyscraper'. *The Times* of London carried the story as a front-page feature and made the building their leading photograph. Good architecture or bad architecture, it was a brilliant piece of public relations.

The strange thing is that AT&T had not realised that there was anything odd about the building until the row blew up, so unaware were they about the climate of architectural debate within which the building was produced, and so charming was Mr Johnson's boardroom performance. They had gone to him on the strength of his reputation as America's *architecte du roi* – a man who could transform you, by your patronage, from a raw businessman into a cultural aristocrat, if you were not that already. To have Philip Johnson take on your commission was like being admitted to court.

In spite of having only taken up architecture at the age of forty, Mr Johnson was already well enough known on the social register to install himself fairly rapidly as palace builder to the most powerful of America's commercial nobility – to business empires like Pennzoil and IDS; to educational fortresses like Harvard and Yale; and to the not so petty monarchies that bridge the gap between the two – Mrs John D. Rockefeller, for example, or the Amon Carter Foundation. Winning a commission from the massive AT&T company only made his claim official, like Bernini being commissioned by the Pope 350 years earlier.

If Johnson is America's royal architect, however, he is also its royal fool – brilliant and paradoxical, an idolater and an iconoclast – who thumbs his nose at every doctrine of his own age only to flirt outrageously with the doctrines of every other. In 1949, for example, in the 32-acre grounds of his Victorian home in New Canaan, Connecticut, he built himself a house out of glass, apparently in homage to Mies van der Rohe whom he had worked with briefly, and all but worshipped for the previous twenty years. But as soon as it was acclaimed the very Parthenon of American Modernism, Johnson announced to the tinkling of his cap and bells that it actually drew on sixteen historical sources as well, from the Parthenon itself to Karl Friedrich Schinkel, Claude Ledoux, Kazimir Malevich, and Theo van Doesburg. 'One cannot *not* know history,' he teased.

Living in a glass house has never stopped Philip Johnson from throwing stones. Having been one of the first to drag American architecture into the twentieth century in the 1930s, he was also among the first to abandon it. Thirteen years after building the Glass House, he added a miniature folly that reached out like a jetty into his private lake. It was a pavilion of columns just six feet high, inspired by a sixteenth-century *tempietto* built by a Duke of Mantua for his retinue of dwarfs – a reflection, perhaps, of what Johnson privately thought of his frequent house guests. The design consisted of a colonnade which, like himself, could turn and face in any direction, and whose ceiling he decorated in gold leaf, recalling – he insisted – the great mosque of Córdoba, a building with which it could hardly have had anything else in common.

As with the folly, fellow architects were baffled and enraged at his design for AT&T, though not altogether surprised. His work, and that of his partner since 1967, John Burgee, is widely regarded as trivial, decadent and irresponsible, making him the best-hated architect in the world – an accolade quoted with Philip Johnson's approval in the glossiest coffee-table book of his work.

Johnson revels in the intense disapproval which he inflames in the hearts of many members of his profession. Having once ruled as America's high priest of steel and glass, he now parades his loss of faith with brazen enthusiasm. He regards his AT&T Building as the logical outcome of a career that first came to public attention with the Seagram Building on Park Avenue, on which he collaborated with Mies van der Rohe in the mid-1950s. With its floor-to-ceiling windows, its continuous external framework of bronze mullions, and its spartan – or perhaps Athenian – elevator lobby and plaza, the Seagram is still, after twenty-five years, the very essence of urbanity in the hubbub of New York; at the age of seventy-nine, so is Philip Johnson, who has his office on its 36th and 37th floors.

His reception suite is cool and grey, and furnished with Mies' Barcelona chairs and Frank Stella paintings. Philip Johnson completes the picture in his heavy, round, Le Corbusier glasses. He picks and pecks his way around the office like a wiry starling, restlessly shooting his cuffs and adjusting his tie. He is, as ever, brisk, spry, and impatient. Friends who knew him when he was at the newly-founded Museum of Modern Art in the 1930s remember him barely able to stop himself running round the corridors. As a student, too, his energy was irrepressible. In his seven years as a Harvard undergraduate – a period in which he was dogged with nervous ill-health – he majored in philosophy and took a minor in Greek, while nursing a secret passion for mathematical physics. And this was after giving up his ambition of becoming a concert pianist. At this stage in his career, his ambitions seem to have outstripped his abilities to achieve them.

Johnson: I'm not a polymath. All the ideas of becoming a concert pianist are very much like the little boy who wants to be a fireman when he's young. It was just one of those rebellious desires: we all hate our families so much, you see, that I expressed mine in a different way.

The philosophy part was a little more serious. I was a great friend of the philosopher Alfred North Whitehead, who was such a strong character that I was led along by him and the men around him into intellectual pursuits which I was very, very poor at.

I remember asking Mr Whitehead once why I got a B – he never gave Bs – and he said 'Well, I only have two kinds of marks: one that's nice and one that can't make it.' And it was quite clear that Mr Whitehead thought I couldn't make it, so I quit.

Games: If it was an intellectual interest, why did you not turn to the purest of the arts – painting and sculpture – rather than to architecture which requires more compromising?

Johnson: I can't paint, I can't draw, I'm not as interested in them as I was in architecture. My mother was interested in art. She taught art in public schools and had a collection of slides in the home. But the only thing that caught my eye was architecture. The turning point in my life was 1928, and a trip up the Nile and to Athens. I realised that the only thing I looked at was the architecture, not the sculpture.

Games: But in your recent writings, you do relate architecture very closely to sculpture. You talk about it as a sculptural form.

Johnson: That's clear, isn't it? Architecture has a relation to sculpture in that it's three-dimensional, and you look at it, and it *is* art. After all, it was a sculptor who built the Parthenon. I was just reading last night how Phidias really had more influence on Pericles than Ictinus did. So sculpture was very close to architecture in those days. The *entasis* on the Parthenon columns was certainly a sculptural element. And so of course I've always been interested in sculpture, but only as it applies to architecture.

I'm working on a tower now, the Rose Tower. I think I can make it a reference to de Chirico and have some fun. But that's painting, so you see I'm interested in painting too, as long as the painter's name is de Chirico.

Games: You bask in history. Where does it come from? You weren't studying history at Harvard.

Johnson: No, I never took a course in history. I've never taken a course in art. I don't think college is any good. Universities should be left out. As far as teaching is concerned, Harvard was absolutely useless.

Games: You were an architecture critic, and then you went on to become an architect. Did your liberal education not provide you with something which other architects didn't have?

Johnson: Well, I say it didn't; everybody else says of course it did, and that I shouldn't misjudge the influences upon me. All right then, it did. I don't care – whichever is true.

You see, to me, my life is a perfectly straight line. To everybody else, there couldn't be anything crookeder. My early interest in [right-wing] politics for instance,[1] my interest in farming, my interest in music or philosophy – all these twists and turns that I managed to fit into my career are just too peculiar for words, but they're not peculiar to me. They're a perfectly straight line. I went from criticism to architecture because it interested me more. I noticed I was designing things while I was being a critic. I did a watch for my sister which she still wears, and quite a handsome dress for her début. I didn't know much about bias cutting and you do have to know about bias cutting if you're going to be a fashion person. So I wasn't very good at that either. But all those things that critics can't do, I found myself doing impulsively.

Games: Could you have pursued it?

Johnson: Oh Lord, no, I wasn't any good; no, that isn't true: I didn't want to. By then I got interested in architecture – which to me is the only real expression of three-dimensional work. I can't understand why anybody can be anything but an architect. I suppose that sounds narrow-minded, but I don't care. I think narrow-mindedness is very important. Have you ever seen a real craftsman in ivory or in weaving or in embroidery, or a farmer who is so concerned with the growing of things that he bursts into tears

[1]Philip Johnson was an adherent of fascism for a brief time in the 1930s, and would make public speeches in the southern states, urging farmers towards political and agricultural self-sufficiency. He was in Berlin in the summer and autumn leading up to the outbreak of the Second World War, and his allegiances were widely enough known for him to be mistaken for a collaborator by the American authorities at the time. It was, however, no more than youthful naïvety which he quickly got over, he now says.

when his field gets flooded? I mean, passions and narrowness of that kind are what we lack in America. We've much too much liberalism – 'let the little dears express themselves'. That never got anybody anywhere. It's the narrowness of the laser beam that gets things cut.

Philip Johnson discovered what the laser beam of passion could do in 1919 when, at the age of thirteen, his mother took him to see Chartres Cathedral. It made a huge impression upon him. Years later, he told an audience of students that he would rather sleep in the nave of Chartres with the nearest toilets six blocks away than in a Harvard student hostel [designed by Walter Gropius, then Harvard's Professor of Architecture] with back-to-back bathrooms! So much for functional architecture.

Fortunately, he has never needed to sleep in cathedrals or in utility housing. His lawyer father provided him with a substantial private income by giving him stock in Alcoa, the Aluminium Company of America, which he had once been presented with in lieu of a fee. At the age of twenty-four, it made young Philip a good deal wealthier than his father, himself the owner of a 3000-acre farm in Cleveland, Ohio. It gave him the means and the cast of mind, until recently, to keep returning to Chartres and other Continental haunts for his architectural references, like a New York *grande dame* on a shopping spree at Harrods.

Johnson spent the 1930s as a historian and museum curator. Having graduated from Harvard, he met the art historian Henry-Russell Hitchcock with whom he spent the summer of 1930 driving round Europe, *doing* modern architecture, and meeting many of its pioneers – J. J. P. Oud in Holland, Le Corbusier in France, and – prophetically – Mies van der Rohe and Walter Gropius in Germany, before either of them had emigrated to the United States. Back in New York that autumn, Johnson was invited to set up and fund a department of architecture at the new Museum of Modern Art that his friend Alfred Barr had established the year before. Before long, Barr, Hitchcock and Johnson were all at work promoting their new enthusiasm.

They saw themselves as the scourge of the conservative American establishment. During the annual exhibition of the Architectural League in 1931, they hired a sandwich man to stand outside the League's doors and advertise their own *Salon des Refusés*. The League reacted by attempting to have the man arrested. In 1932, Johnson held an exhibition of modern European architecture based on what he had seen on holiday two years earlier. Barr wrote the catalogue, and Hitchcock and Johnson expanded it into the book *The International Style*, published later that year. In 1934, they created another society scandal by displaying ball-bearings and electric toasters in an exhibition of machine art.

They were obviously having a good time. What they were doing was radical, but it was also wild and high-spirited. On Johnson's money, they could afford to be frivolous. What Alfred Barr was calling 'the International Style' was known in Europe as 'the Modern Movement'. There was a significant difference. The original political intentions of this design ideology had been converted in America into a consumer aesthetic – what the architect Peter Eisenman has described as 'a transformation from a pluralistic conception of the good society into an individualistic model of the good life'.

Johnson: I had a lot of fun travelling round Europe. And that's how I found out that I did have critical ability in architecture. I thought Mies van de Rohe and Le Corbusier were much better than Adolf Loos and Bruno Taut, let's say. But in those days, nobody could tell the difference. Nobody had heard of Mies. Even my colleague Henry-Russell Hitchcock with whom I wrote the book didn't see what I saw in Mies. Mies was too simple for him. Le Corbusier was much more painterly, much more expressive in his shapes, and Mies seemed almost nothing, which of course is exactly what he wanted to be. But I didn't mind the almost nothing, the less-is-more attitude.

Games: You became associated with Mies later. What did he think of your interpretation of him? Did he feel you were a threat?

Johnson: In no way was I a threat. I was a pupil and a worshipper. He felt ill at ease in the States, he always felt more German, and when I offered to work with him on the Seagram Building, he was delighted because he felt that I could pave the way for him.[1] And it's true – I could and I did.

Games: But did he want to be worshipped for the things you were worshipping him for?

Johnson: Oh yes. We talked for hours. He liked to drink a great

[1]Philip Johnson worked on the Seagram commission with Mies van der Rohe. Samuel Bronfman, head of the Seagram Corporation, had already got a provisional skyscraper design from Charles Luckman Associates in 1954 when his daughter Phyllis Lambert intervened and badgered him to build something more modern. He agreed if she could find a suitable architect. Philip Johnson, whom she had met at Alfred Barr's, drew up a list of possibles, from which she finally chose Mies. But Mies, who worked in Chicago, had no New York office, and a friend of Bronfman's nominated Johnson to be his New York base.

deal and after the third Martini we could always get a flow going. 'Let's have another!' was his most famous remark; it's the one he's always quoted for and it really was a daily occurrence. There would be long, three-hour lunches and then a flood of conversation would occur.

Games: But he once stormed out of your house in New Canaan, never to return.

Johnson: That's true, by Jove. I asked him an intellectual question – he was not an intellectual. I asked him what he saw in the Dutch Art-Nouveau architect Berlage, his guru; what shapes did he think inspired his work? Because Berlage used masonry walls and an iron roof, and used glass in a most peculiar way and his buildings really looked Romanesque, and what did he see in them? And he got up and he said: 'I'm leaving. I'll never come back.' And I thought he was kidding so I went on. And he said: 'I don't think you heard me. I'm not spending the night.' There was no place to send him, there were no hotels there. So we got him a room at a friend of mine's house. It was most embarrassing.

But there I was rude because I pinned him down to an intellectual point which he was not prepared to answer. He was a 'dese und dose' man. He just said: 'I think we do it "*dis*" way', and that was the way it was done. But he couldn't anymore explain how or why than the man in the moon. At the same time, he had a love of St Thomas and the feeling that beauty is merely the reflection of truth.

Games: How does that operate in your own work? Do you apply the same sort of intellectual disciplines there?

Johnson: Of course not because I don't believe in principles. He did, you see. He was a man of deep principles – a lapsed Catholic but nevertheless a deep Catholic in his thinking. He felt very strongly that the only way towards an abstract thing called Beauty with a capital B, if you please, was truth, because if you built truly, you built beautifully. Beauty was truth and truth was beauty – a thing I've always hated John Keats for, and always will, because as Nietzsche very properly replied: 'Art is with us that we not perish from truth.' In other words, truth just gets in the way and you don't have nothin'. Art is artifice, the opposite of truth: it's invention, it's lying, it's cheating the eye, it's subverting the psyche. That's what art is. But not to Mies. Mies said: 'If it's well built, honest to its structure, if it looks like a building, that's what matters.'

One of my buildings that he didn't mind looking at was my

house down the street here [the Rockefeller residence at the Museum of Modern Art] and he said of it: 'Das ist gebaut.' In other words, that building is really *built*. That was his highest form of praise. Of course I just laughed, because if a building didn't look built, it would look much more amusing, wouldn't it?

Games: Did you know that before you became an architect, at the time when you were still only a critic?

Johnson: Of course, and before that when I was studying philosophy. It was obvious to me that Relativism was the only absolute, that change was the only thing in life to look to, and that the truth-and-beauty business – and Plato, don't forget – was quite a big enemy too. You see, abstraction – the fact that the Ideal was something that existed – was nonsense. Relativism and change were the only things that were any good.

Games: You've often spoken about your earliest architectural experiences in the terms that people use to talk about religious awakenings.

Johnson: It was a completely religous feeling when I saw the Parthenon. I wrote once that there was a pre-Parthenon Philip Johnson and a post-Parthenon Philip Johnson. I felt renewed, the way President Carter must have felt when he was reborn. Since I never was reborn, I'm not sure what that means but that's the way I felt.

Games: Were you ever attracted to religion?

Johnson: Oh yes. When one was young, one went and got reborn at a great Mass or rally. It's a very strange feeling. But I realised it was just a feeling because the next morning I felt quite the same – rang out with the same old sins – delightfully!

Games: What happens when you do a church, because you've done quite a number?

Johnson: Well that's the most interesting job in the world because you want to increase the feeling of religiosity and of dedication to a God, whoever you may happen to want to believe in. But it's much the same as a concert hall. To me, music is much finer in a fine visual setting and I enjoy concert halls much more if they're good architecture. The same applies to a church. One of my earlier, silly remarks was: 'If I could become a Catholic, I would go and live in the city of Chartres; if I lived in the city of Chartres, I would certainly become a Catholic.' In other words, the experience of being bathed in the light from those coloured windows would make a very good Roman Catholic of anyone, it seems to me. That's why I can't but go alone to Chartres – because anyone I go with can't possibly have the same feelings I do, and I get jarred by their lack of reaction.

Games: When you build a church – and you are now doing a cathedral as well[1] – who do you direct the building to? A Christian architect would be delivering the building to God, but in the absence of that . . . ?

Johnson: Well, in my dedicatory speech, I made a speech about God. It seemed very much with me at the time, so I didn't feel I was being totally hypocritical. And I said that the terrible thing is that our generation does not build for perhaps the greatest aims in the world which is the greater glory of God. *Ad maiorem gloriam Dei* should be above every door of every church because to glorify God and to raise the level of emotions of the people that want to kneel is certainly what I'm on Earth for. So in building a church I really feel that I'm doing something, but I don't think there needs to be anything out there for me to get the same feeling they get.

Philip Johnson's remarks closely echo those that Ruskin made in *The Seven Lamps of Architecture*, the work that so influenced the architects and painters of his day. 'Architecture,' said Ruskin, 'is the art which so disposes and adorns the edifices raised by man that the sight of them might contribute to his mental health, power, and pleasure.'

In an attack on architectural teaching in 1954, Johnson adapted the title of Ruskin's book in order to hit out at what he regarded at the time as the seven *crutches* of architecture, in particular of student architecture. These included the crutch of pretty drawing, the crutch of functionalism, the crutch of treating cheapness as a virtue, of servility to the client, and of taking too much interest in the structure of the building. A sixth crutch was that of novelty for its own sake. Johnson argued for tradition instead, quoting what Mies van der Rohe had once said to him – that it was better to be good than to be original.

On the other hand, there was one crutch – the crutch of history – which Johnson discounted at the time as being no longer applicable. 'History doesn't bother us very much now,' he said,

---

[1]The Garden Grove community church – or 'Crystal Cathedral' – in California, now complete.

'but in the old days, you could always rely on books. You could say: "What do you mean, you don't like my tower? There it is in Wren."' With history back in vogue, it is a crutch he frequently uses today in his own work. This does not mean that he feels himself any closer to Ruskin.

Johnson: The trouble with Ruskin was that he was a moralist. He was not a Nietzschean. He liked Gothic architecture and *bad* Gothic architecture, and did not like great architecture which was that of the Renaissance. To Ruskin, Renaissance architecture was a sham. 'The pilaster was a lie,' Goethe said; to me, pilasters are very important wall decorations to give form to what are otherwise just walls. So I could never agree with Ruskin except about his politics, which no one else agrees with but me.

Games: You have said that everyone ought to have a definition of architecture. Do you have such a definition?

Johnson: No, no. My definition would be non-definition, you see. It was much easier in Mies' days when Mies' discipline was mine. I swallowed him hook, line and sinker and so I felt that his was the clue to help me, since I was a rather modest practitioner. I never thought of myself as a great architect; I still don't. I don't think there *is* any great architecture right now. I think we're in a waiting period, which is normal – we don't always have master periods.

The English still call the early International Style the 'Heroic' period of modern architecture, that is, when Le Corbusier and Mies were at their best and formed a duet of great architecture which is still an absolute standard. Mies' Seagram Building is still the finest building in New York, his *capo laboro*, although I've built several buildings here myself. But there's no question in my mind that we're not living in that heroic period anymore. In those days, you could say *why* the details on the Seagram façades were better than the details on his Chicago buildings, or why his placing of the Seagram on Park Avenue was better than anything he did elsewhere. And you could say about Le Corbusier that his [monastery at] Ronchamp was maybe the greatest piece of architecture of our century. Those things became clear; nothing is clear today. There is nobody – certainly none of my contemporaries – who can reach that standard. We're all small little people running around doing our little thing, as Tom Wolfe would put it, hoping that lightning will strike.

You see, Mies had absolute confidence in his God, in his

leadership, in his genius. Frank Lloyd Wright did too. None of us has that feeling. We're all cynics. We're all feeling that there's no choice except a personal one. But that doesn't hurt anything. Goodness gracious, only a short time ago we laughed at the nineteenth century; now *London 1900* [by Alastair Service] is the most popular book on the English bookstalls. Edwardian is the best of England.

Games: Maybe you feel that our view of architecture is now too broad? I mean, you started off by talking about the narrow cutting edge of the laser beam, as if we should be wearing blinkers.

Johnson: I know. You see, consistency is not one of my main points. I think it's a sign of weakness, so I'm not consistent in any way. My work is all over the place in spite of my narrowness of vision.

Games: What about this business of eclecticism that invades your work? Do you not see it now as one of the crutches?

Johnson: No, don't worry about the words. Just say we build any way we please and that my mansarded hotel in Dallas is very different from my Ledoucian – to use Hitchcock's way of talking about Ledoux – school of architecture in Houston, Texas, or my Neiman Marcus store in Honolulu. That's so Ledoux that you think it's out of page 117 of the book. It actually isn't, but it's a perfect example of Ledoux' work. I'm extraordinarily proud of it and I don't mind at all that it's a dead copy or that it isn't Soanean or Schinkelesque or Michelangelesque.

Games: What is it you're enjoying? Architecture, or being an *agent provocateur?*

Johnson: I think that's a fair question and I simply don't know. I'm enjoying life so much that I can stand laughter and even truthful points like the one you may have just made. Hope you didn't. I mean, I hope it isn't true.

All I know is that when I hit a shape that pleases me, I can sing for the rest of the day, and if I'm working on a problem and it doesn't work, I just have to take too many drinks. It's so depressing, I just don't want to face the world. Now that isn't just joking surely, it isn't just leg-pulling or trying to be an *agent provocateur* or trying to *épater le bourgeois*, whatever the French phrase is we have to use these days. It is sincere in its efforts to make beautiful shapes and if I can get them built, it's the greatest satisfaction an artist can have. When you get doubtful of a building just before it goes up, that's sickening, and then of course the worst thing is to finish a building and find it bad. That can really hurt for a long time.

Games: Has that happened?

Johnson: Oh yes, but I don't talk about those. I don't tell you about them and I don't print them.

Games: It's difficult to know whether you're looking for intellectual discipline or not. You are clearly an intellectual man, your references are second to none, your history is superb.

Johnson: No, I think you're wrong, excuse me, I'm shaking my head because I'm not an intellectual, I'm a flibbertigibbet intellectually, I'm frog-minded, my knowledge of history is highly selective. I would not be a scholar or a teacher, I could not write a history book, I could not give a lecture on Michelangelo's later work. I'm an enthusiast, not an intellectual. There's a difference.

When I'm in touch with people like Hitchcock or Vincent Scully or Robert Venturi, I realise that their background of knowledge is far superior to mine. I'm like a child: very enthusiastic, very perceptive in funny ways, and very quick. You see, I do recognise that my mind works five times the speed of other people, which makes them think I'm an intellectual; all it means is that they're slow – that I can see what they mean before they get it out of their mouths.

And I can do the same for architecture. But I'm not a very good critic, I'm a very second-echelon critic. If Scully points something out to me I say 'Why didn't I think of that?' And then in my next speech, there it is, all wrapped up and neatly put. You see, I can talk very, very well but that's just a gift, not a sign of intellectuality. I know an intellectual when I see one – Isaiah Berlin. In the presence of Isaiah I don't talk; he doesn't give you a chance. Chatter, chatter, chatter. 'Ain't that right, Mr Berlin!' said someone to him. There's a real intellectual in any field. I have fun with him in architecture because he doesn't know much about it. I can even make him keep still for two minutes. But that isn't my being an intellectual. He has a mind I would give anything for. In fact my main wish when I was young was to be a mathematical physicist because to me, it was the foreground of knowledge.

Philip Johnson's curiosity about his milieu explains his architecture. He is by nature a collector. His buildings are museums in reverse; instead of containing exhibits, they *are* the exhibit. His

RepublicBank Center in Houston has the roofline of a Baroque Flemish town hall – a speculation on what a twentieth-century Borromini might have done had he ever worked in Antwerp. The arcade of the United Bank Center in downtown Denver is based on the bulging glass crinolines of Decimus Burton's Palm House at Kew. His office development at 33 Maiden Lane in Lower Manhattan is vaguely Scottish, with crenellations and rounded turrets.

The conventional explanation for these features is that they conform to the spirit of eclecticism. But they conform for sound financial reasons. Open-plan offices command the very lowest rate of floor rentals; turrets, corners and other eccentricities which affect the distribution of internal space are a way of increasing the yield. Companies will pay premium rates for offices in which senior executives can 'express' their seniority. In the American commercial world, architectural quality is measured by the number of status symbols it can cram in, and Mr Johnson happily caters for this need.

The same applies to the external appearance of his buildings. Eccentricity pays; it is an up-market substitute for a flashing neon sign. Behind the Rolls-Royce radiator of the AT&T Building, Mr Johnson claims references – crass, but references nevertheless – to the architecture of ancient Rome and of the Renaissance, to Alberti and Brunelleschi, to the Galeria in Milan, to the architects McKim, Mead and White in the 1890s, and to Raymond Hood in the 1930s. There are no artistic reasons why these should apply to a telecommunications company. Mr Johnson just happens to like them, and if he likes them, then his clients do as well.

But the cast of his mind is less dilettante than he would like to suggest. Take the pink granite stonework, for example. Stone masons have not been seen on the streets of New York for fifty years. What made it feasible to employ them was an economic quirk. The rising cost of fuel had led to a reduction in the size of windows in new buildings, and to the use of tinted double-glazing to control the build-up and retention of heat. For both reasons the price of glass had gone up. This meant that, for a while, the cost of stone as a wall covering was able to compete with the cost of glass. Conditions such as these, and the interests of a particularly image-conscious business community, have enabled Philip Johnson to add to his range of architectural styles without needing to assess their implications. Even in his work, he acts like a museum curator.

The 1950s saw him building up an important private collection at his New Canaan estate, though many of the works he bought – mainly Abstract Expressionists – were given as gifts to MOMA in response to requests from Alfred Barr. This made Johnson the Museum's second largest benefactor of paintings, and in turn brought up the value of his own collection. In the 1960s, at the instigation of his friend David Whitney, he began to buy Pop artists – including Andy Warhol, who in turn made Johnson the subject of a screen print – and Minimalist sculptors whose simple geometric forms he began to reflect in his architecture. By then, he had acquired a fine reputation as America's foremost museum architect, so as well as building museums and art galleries, he was also controlling what went into them, and thereby helping many artists on their way to international reputations.

Johnson has frequently helped to direct the course of architectural commissions as well, and many leading architects now talk effusively about his generosity and support; Michael Graves' controversial design for the Portland Public Services Building in Oregon would probably not have been built if Philip Johnson had not intervened to save it. Apart from his influence in the social and commercial sectors, his architecture has also acted as a catalyst on the profession and he himself believes that it was the AT&T Building in particular that legitimised the Portland Building and others like it.[1]

But Philip Johnson has also been called 'the Godfather' because it seems as if so many people are now in his debt that his own position is unassailable. Although he has never had architectural followers – he is thought of by some as a standard bearer without an army – he is at the same time both king and king-maker at the centre of an architectural culture that is rich and getting richer, both artistically and financially.

He no longer holds court at his New Canaan estate as he used to. Instead he presides – or has done in recent years – over private suppers of a self-appointed New York architectural élite, listening to the discussions over dinner and then summing up with his own architectural benediction. He also took the chair at a clandestine meeting called by the planning theorist Leon Krier at the end of 1982, which took place at the University of Virginia, where Krier had been teaching. Its purpose was to invite the world's thirty leading architects, most of whom were American, to sign a petition drawn up by Krier calling for Rome to be rebuilt. Johnson was one of the few who did not sign; he was one of the few who did not need to. His behind-the-scenes political activity requires him to stay more flexible, and therefore more detached, than the others.

[1] See Chapter 2.

Johnson: Yes, I get that from Mies. We are whores and want to be paid as highly as possible for doing what we do best. Therefore we do skyscrapers best – they're the most profitable. If I were looking at it *sub specie aeternitatis*, I would say 'What are you building all those tall, useless buildings for? Why don't you build churches and shrines and things that really count – like cemeteries?' Lutyens could build cemeteries. That's why I admire him above all modern architects, although he was a *late* discovery of mine, not being Modern enough at one time or classical enough at another. But then when he *did* hit me, he made an enormous impression. He could create monuments, and you're moved by monuments.

Games: How important do you think you are in the way architecture has come up?

Johnson: I think I'm important in the way people say I am. I can't judge myself. I'm very helpful to the young. Because I like their work so much, I recommend them and I've gotten jobs for all these people because I want to raise the level of architecture in this country and I'm in a position to do so.

I've got something. I suppose the AT&T Building [was] the most influential unbuilt building in the world. The only building to be on the front page of the London *Times* must be something. AT&T made it possible for Michael Graves to become accepted as a 'classicist' – although he did it himself; only an artist can make his own work. But people would look at a Graves drawing with classical columns and not shudder. After he'd seen that the largest company in the world (AT&T's larger than most countries, bigger than Sweden, you see) had chosen that kind of building, it meant something. And therefore it was very helpful to Michael. And I think he changed. He was a Modern architect before, rather good but nowhere as good as he is now as a classical architect. I'm very proud of that. I'm very proud of being accepted by the kids. At this conference we had down at the University of Virginia a few weeks ago, I was the only old man. Very proud of that, 'cos Bucky [Buckminster Fuller] wasn't there. I was, and so we had fun.

Games: Can you talk us through the AT&T Building?

Johnson: AT&T is perhaps not very pretty when you look at it but it's very important from the point of view of city planning, from the point of view of the pedestrian. As you walk along the street, it is supported by enormous piers that haven't been seen since Michelangelo. They're fake, of course, because everything now is held up by glue and steel and odd little unarchitectural things like that. These granite columns are placed very close together – more of a hypostyle Egyptian hall than anything else. And you wander in, and you're bounced from column to column – there's no glass, there's no entrance, there's no lobby – so the feeling you get of AT&T isn't what you see in the pictures. It's a feeling of majesty, that here are great hunks of solid stone that give you a feeling of olden times, whatever that is.

And then you walk in front of it and in front of it is the highest archway you've ever seen in your life. It's 110 feet high, but it's only 110 feet across from sidewalk to sidewalk, so you look like this, you tip your head up, and you can catch the top of the arch and it is quite, somebody said, awe-inspiring – it is even to me. Well then I've done something, you see. I don't care if I got the arch from the Pazzi Chapel, which is an entirely different scale and an entirely different purpose.

I've given the whole of the interior to the public. No lobby, no nothing, just one little cell in the middle of the great block. In that cell is the cult statue, it's the golden representation of the telephone company. They always used it as their symbol and like the Romans carry their *lares* and *penates* with them from home to home, I insisted on carrying this sculpture from the top of their old building into this cell of the new. The relation of that sculpture to the cell is very much like the relation of the chryselephantine Athene in the cell at the Parthenon. She was much over-scaled; she almost hit the ceiling. Well, so does this statue. It fills the cell. You walk into this cell with the symbol being the biggest thing in the world and there are a couple of elevators. That's never been done before in the history of skyscrapers. So I've already done something, you see.

The second thing that happens in AT&T is that you see it from down Sixth Avenue or from across East River, and there is this amazingly strong top. There are not enough tops in New York. In modern architecture, of course, we just cut them off flat. That's useless; you've got to have a tower. So we invented a pediment but it's a pediment on the wrong side of the building,[1] and then we just cut out a hole. The top surprised everybody. They thought it was ugly and mannerist, and whatever bad words they could think of. Well it isn't. It's strong, and as you pass it in an aeroplane or from a distance, you can see through the building. That's a nice little shift of things which you can't get from the model or from pictures.

---

[1] In classical architecture, the pediment appears above the short façade of a building. The pediment at the AT&T appears above the long façade.

And it's been very well received, I'm glad to say, and people are changing their minds one after another,[1] and now it's finally built it doesn't look funny or ugly, so it's been very nice.

Games: You talk about the building's majesty. Why would you want to give majesty to a telephone company?

Johnson: I'd give majesty to an out-house. I've never been to a majestic out-house. I hope to some day build one. Of course we don't use them much anymore, except in rural parts of the United States. They've never seen one in England, I imagine.

Games: How happy do you feel with commercial clients?

Johnson: Perfect. I'm very commercial myself and I find they're just as intelligent. They're looked down on by socialists of various kinds and socialists are looked down on by them. I mean, I think we all like to have someone to look down on. The English can look down on the Americans, and they have plenty to look down on, but we also have a chance to look down on the British. They're not doing so confoundedly well themselves nowadays. So that gives you a sense of superiority which is what keeps you going, isn't it? The commercial people in this world – the really rich, the really successful and managerial types – have a justifiable sense of pride in their work, and majesty is what they need to celebrate it. But I would do it for Lenin too. I don't care.

Games: But there have been times when you seem to have been pitted pretty strongly against commercial architects and their concerns.

Johnson: Intellectually, of course, I would be a socialist. Even Bentham may have said something right – 'the greatest happiness for the greatest number'. What I would like to build is housing, what I would like to build is cities, where people could live happier lives.

Games: It's said that you turn away 90 per cent of commissions.

Johnson: I know it is, but why not exaggerate? If it were 10 per cent it would be very high. Turn away a great big $200 million building?

Games: How do you decide which ones to take on?

Johnson: Whether the client is really interested in architecture, whether he really wants to create something, and whether he's really serious in going through with it.

[1]See Jonathan Barnett on p. 73.

Games: The fact that you are choosing them at the same time as being chosen by them makes you just as much the patron as they are.

Johnson: Yes, my only good client is of course myself. All my good works are out at my place in Connecticut. I'm planning a new one now. I test things on myself. It isn't fair to try arcuated temples and things on clients that pay for them. You should have fun at your own expense and then if it works, it gets into the stream of your work.

Games: I have a quotation from Henry-Russell Hitchcock who said that you started off as a very timid designer – that you were almost excessively distrustful of your own powers of invention. Was that the case?

Johnson: Yes it was. He did. And I was. And then he added – have you got the rest of the quote there? – that I became a very strong architect, started using strong shapes, maybe too strong. I don't quite remember that part of the quote. But he never thought much of me, doesn't think much of me as an architect. He doesn't consider me up with the good architects, and I don't consider myself that way because I really don't care. I'm doing the best I can, the thing that excites me most. I'm the happiest man in the world, I'm doing what I want, and earning money which is also a nice American thing – Americans judge you by how much money you make, so I'm quite all right, thank you – so I'm successful in every definition of that word, and that is so incredible to me that I just rejoice every day of being alive.

Sir Edwin Lutyens:
The Empire Strikes Back

You can put an exhibition into a building; you cannot put a
building into an exhibition. Which is why of all the arts, exhibitions about architecture are the most difficult, and perhaps the
least rewarding, to stage or to visit; the exhibits are always a
substitute for the real thing.

This resistance by architecture to the art gallery and the
museum has helped to prevent it from being consecrated as an
art not just in the mind of the public but in the mind of the galleries
themselves. This may have been to architecture's advantage
especially when, as today, we find it difficult to define art as
anything more than 'that which can be shown in an exhibition'.
The fact that buildings can only properly be seen in their natural
settings means that unlike painting and sculpture, they refuse to
pay homage to the tyranny of the gallery.

In spite of this, exhibitions are increasingly being held which do
show and reduce the art of architecture. Buildings are presented
through photography, drawings and models – media which draw

attention to themselves at architecture's expense. Such exhibitions are so obviously unsatisfactory that only someone with something else on his mind would want to put one on. One group that certainly had something else on its mind was the planning committee of the Edwin Lutyens exhibition in 1981.

Sir Edwin Lutyens had been the favourite country-house architect of the Edwardians. A prodigiously early starter, he set up his own practice in 1889 at the age of 20. By 1900 he already had one of the busiest practices in the country. He was additionally lucky in being taken up by the publisher of *Country Life*, Edward Hudson, for whom he rebuilt Lindisfarne Castle in 1903 and provided new offices in Tavistock Street in London in 1904. Hudson published each new building by Lutyens in the pages of his magazine, thereby converting many of his readers into clients. They were men of wealth, and in some cases power, and they wanted to see their sense of their own eminence confirmed in the property they owned. Lutyens gave them opulent, imposing, characterful buildings – traditional enough in appearance to suggest an architectural pedigree but with flashes of individuality breaking through the conventional constraints.

During the course of his career, Lutyens accumulated praise and honour. In 1918, at the age of 49, he was knighted. In 1921 he won the King's Gold Medal for Architecture and in 1938 he became President of the Royal Academy – a post he held until his death in 1944. With his passing, however, his reputation quickly slumped and his former popularity was forgotten. An era had come to an end and in the post-war climate of rebuilding and the Welfare State, his work seemed indulgent and irrelevant. When the architecture critic Robert Furneaux-Jordan was invited to speak about him at a meeting of the Architectural Association in 1959, he announced that he felt like an atheist giving an address from the balcony of St Peter's. Even Lutyens' son Robert – himself an architect – had difficulty in the 1950s in coming to terms with the absence of social concerns in his father's work and his lack of faith in what the new age had had to offer: technology, secondary education and municipal planning.

Lutyens' work was too attractive, however, to be ignored by all and throughout the years when modern architecture was at its most doctrinaire, a core of supporters stood by, waiting to say 'I told you so'. They seemed to have the perfect opportunity in 1969 – the year of Lutyens' centenary. The previous year had seen the collapse of Ronan Point, an event which marked a watershed of disaffection with high-rise buildings and slab blocks. Attempts were made to hold a Lutyens exhibition which would celebrate not just the man and his architecture but the historicist backwater that he had been a part of. The Royal Academy seemed an appropriate place to hold it, not just because of Lutyens' association with the building but because of its status as a symbol of architectural and political conservatism. But the attempt failed, as did fresh attempts in 1980, because the planning committee for the exhibition had misread the Academy's conservatism. The Academy felt that architecture shows were too difficult to mount, of only limited public or artistic interest, and therefore financially unappealing compared with the more expensive but more remunerative international blockbusters of famous paintings.

The Academy's disdain for architecture ought to have been especially embarrassing during the eight-year presidency, from 1976 to 1984, of the architect Sir Hugh Casson. He was in fact taken to task for his lack of initiative at the Academy's summer banquet in 1981 by the American architect Philip Johnson, but to no effect. This was hardly surprising. From its birth in 1768 until the birth of the Royal Institute of British Architects in 1824, the Royal Academy was the sole representative body of the architectural profession, as it was of painters and sculptors. In time, however, it was eclipsed by the RIBA, to the extent that it has now given up its claim to represent architecture in all but name. Apart from having a small architectural section in its summer shows, its constitutional commitment to architecture has ceased to exist. Its architecture school was closed down after almost two centuries in 1965 and its last exclusively architectural exhibition was held in 1976 – a memorial to Raymond Erith, a neo-Georgian architect who had died three years earlier.

The attempt to stage the Lutyens show at the Royal Academy therefore represented more than just a wish to present Lutyens in a building he had been associated with and one with elegant, spacious rooms; it was also a remarkably reactionary attempt to move the clock back by by-passing the RIBA and its mercenary pragmatism and restore architecture to the clubbish, gentlemanly surroundings of Piccadilly.

The Academy's rejection of these overtures came as a blow. It showed that by 1980, the new Toryism in architecture had still not managed to convince the old guard of the political programme which lay behind their enthusiasm for Lutyens: the wish to reverse the march of progress in architecture and institute a return to Victorian values. The motivation for this programme was simple enough – and simple-minded: that because certain kinds of modern architecture were felt not to have worked, traditional architecture was the only alternative. This is the thinking that Lutyens was held to embody. His work was clearly old-fashioned, not forward-looking; it was craftsmanly, not mass-produced; it was emotional, not theoretical; it was popular, not arcane; and – perhaps most important – it was English, not international.

The embarrassing thing for the committee was that the contemporary revaluation of Lutyens as a figure of interest and a unique English phenomenon had taken place not in conservative English circles but among more independent-minded foreigners – notably from the two countries which had done most for modern architecture: Germany and America. It was the German art historian Nikolaus Pevsner who, in a climate largely hostile to Lutyens, had first tried to reassess his career. In an essay written in 1951, he confessed to being irritated by Lutyens' architectural jokes – the famous disappearing pilasters on the Midland Bank in the City of London, for example, which vanish into the wall like the grin on the Cheshire Cat – and wondered whether such an architect could possibly be regarded as 'great'. His answer was that Lutyens was a paradoxical figure in whom wit and whimsy had to be taken seriously because they were a reflection of qualities intrinsic to him and to England. Pevsner salvaged Lutyens' reputation by equating individual and national characteristics.

In 1913, Lawrence Weaver had also made an association between the individuality and inherent Englishness of Lutyens' houses, but had chosen very different evidence in support of these qualities. He had been struck by the charm of the work, its degree of craftsmanship, its sense of balance and wholeness, and – surprisingly now – its modernity. He went along with Lutyens' novelties and tricks as long as they were treated with discretion, but not the 'constructive jests' which he dismissed: '[These] belong to Mr Lutyens' *juvenilia* and have long been abandoned for a more serious outlook.'

The fact that Pevsner was able not just to come to some reconciliation with the unacceptable side of Lutyens but to turn it into a virtue was no accident. As a young historian in Germany, he had done research into the eccentric Jesuitical art of the early sixteenth century – an art which had taken outrageous liberties with the conventions of classicism without ultimately rejecting them. He was therefore well placed to deal with Lutyens' mannerisms when he found them.

Pevsner's reading of Lutyens caught on more quickly in America than in Britain. A small centenary exhibition of his work at the

RIBA in 1969 – a substitute for the failed attempt at the Royal Academy – was a very minor affair in the calendar of that year. Far more significant was a companion article written in the Institute's journal by the American architect and critic Robert Venturi in reply to an earlier savaging of Lutyens by two English architects, Alison and Peter Smithson.

Lutyens also benefited from American sentimentality about England. The same spirit which led American television audiences to regard Edwardian costume dramas like *Upstairs Downstairs*, *The Duchess of Duke Street* and *Edward VII* as serious cultural achievements led American architects not just to enjoy Edwardian architecture but to wish to absorb it into their work.

The vogue for Edwardiana made it easier for American architects to retreat into decorative self-expression in the face of more complex challenges to their imaginations. A new vocabulary of watchwords also began to emerge: *irreverence, wit, paradox* – words now especially associated with Lutyens. With them came an appreciation that for architectural paradox to operate as a device, and for expectations to be aroused and then confounded, there had to be an ordered language of architecture which architects could refer to and which the public could share. The logical conclusion was to argue for the restitution of traditional styles of building in which a formal set of rules bound aesthetic and technical considerations together. Hence, a cycle of appreciation that had begun by interpreting Lutyens as a rebel against convention came round to using him as a figurehead for its revival.

Among the most conservative of the new American radicals – or the most radical of the new American conservatives – was Allan Greenberg, whose own designs were very much in the Lutyens style. Greenberg pressed the Museum of Modern Art in New York to mount a modest but, as it turned out, influential exhibition about Lutyens in 1978. The British Embassy in Washington – a Lutyens building – celebrated the event with a dinner and it was there that the idea for a major retrospective in London was again mooted. This was strongly supported by Philip Johnson and when the Royal Academy failed to deliver, members of the Lutyens exhibition planning committee took advantage of Johnson's invitation as guest speaker at the Academy's annual summer banquet in 1981 and instructed him to attack Sir Hugh Casson's presidency – referred to earlier – for its loss of nerve on architecture.

After the failure of this initiative, the exhibition planning committee turned to the Arts Council, in spite of some antipathy among them to the Arts Council's existence, to its policies, and to the fact that any exhibition it put on would have to be housed in the Council's own exhibition space – the Hayward Gallery on London's South Bank – a modern concrete bunker rather different in spirit from Lutyens' work. Somewhat to their surprise, and not entirely to their pleasure, the Arts Council agreed. This meant that not only had Lutyens been usurped by German Modernists and American sentimentalists; he had now been given the imprimatur by English populists. It was a sour victory.

The exhibition at the Hayward was compromised in other ways. Apart from the writer Mary Links, Lutyens' youngest daughter and biographer, and Margaret Richardson of the Drawings Collection of the British Architectural Library, the 1981 planning committee were fogeys to a man: the writer and former pub architect Roderick Gradidge, the architectural correspondent of the *Financial Times* Colin Amery, and the architectural historians David Watkin and Gavin Stamp – specialists, respectively, in late English classicism and the architecture of Victorian and Edwardian England. As the idea for an exhibition became a reality, however, additional manpower had to be co-opted. These included the disgraced Sir Hugh Casson on whom hopes for a Burlington House exhibition had foundered; the architects Peter Inskip, author of a monograph on Lutyens, and Piers Gough, who was to design the show; Nicholas Taylor, a founding member of the Victorian Society but now involved with housing association and planning matters in South London; and Jane Brown, a landscape designer.

The co-opted wets brought an unwanted balance to the committee, sparking off several arguments over interpretation and intentions that were finally reflected in the chaotic incoherence of the exhibition. This opened with Lutyens' student drawings, photographs of his early cottage designs, a crude reconstruction by trainee brickies of a fireplace he had designed and a rather unconvincing stone terrace on which stood a copy of a garden bench he had created for Gertrude Jekyll. It ended with three lacklustre recreations of Lutyens' rooms approached by way of a wobbly brick floor bedded in loose sand. Lutyens' great model of Liverpool Cathedral was also shown, but the rest of his work was for the most part represented by old black-and-white photographs from *Country Life* and new colour photographs specially taken to document the present state of his buildings. If the overall effect was one of carelessness, it was difficult not to wonder whether this was not an indication of the pique of those organisers for whom the mere fact of being seen at the Hayward was an indignity they wished to forget as quickly as possible.

The hard core members were at least able to disassociate themselves from the exhibition in their writings. The exhibition catalogue allowed them to contribute essays which spelled out their particular enthusiasms in their own terms; many of them also took the opportunity to bring out their own books and to publish appreciations of Lutyens in the press.

The general tone of this writing had been established in 1977 by David Watkin who asserted in his book *Morality and Architecture* that Lutyens was one of the two or three most brilliant architects England had ever produced – a point he presented as axiomatic, but which the architectural historian Reyner Banham described in his *TLS* review of the book as 'preposterous'. Dr Watkin also compared the absence of Lutyens' name in Pevsner's *An Outline of European Architecture* to the Soviet Communist Party's deletion of politically unacceptable figures from documentary photographs.

Four years later, this confrontational silliness had become endemic. A re-issued edition of Lawrence Weaver's book on Lutyens announced on its dust jacket that 'the fact that [Modernism] dominated the twenties and thirties accounts for Lutyens' obscurity at that time. Now that the modern school has exploited its ideas to their logical but sterile end, the durability of Lutyens' work can clearly be seen.'

This idea was taken further by Roderick Gradidge in *The Times*. Such was the inhumanity of modern architecture and so overshadowed was Lutyens' genius by it, he said, that by the time of the Second World War, 'leftist intellectuals' were able to press their beliefs onto the unsuspecting British soldiery, encouraging them to decimate German cities, towns and palaces, quite possibly out of sheer architectural spite. He also observed that Germany's unparalleled destruction had been brought upon it, ironically, by a man who loved architecture, and went on to equate the schemes of Hitler and Speer for a new Berlin with the schemes for a new London with which Lutyens occupied himself during his last, dying, wartime years.

Lutyens was also used as a focus for a general anxiety about the future – an anxiety which expressed itself in a wave of patriotism which had no other outlet (this was before the Falklands campaign). 'Lutyens dominated British architecture in one of those periods when, like British music of that time, it was admired throughout the world,' wrote Mr Gradidge somewhat misleadingly. He added that Lutyens' Cenotaph in Whitehall had taken on a deeper symbolism as a national monument not just to the dead of the Great War but to the passing of 'a world which, for all its unfairness and misery, nonetheless offered to more people than at any other time a secure vision of settled peace and ultimate prosperity'. The Lutyens phenomenon was therefore bound up with an aggressive nostalgia for a time when Britannia was ascendant, a third of the globe red, the world in awe, the servants below stairs, and the doubters scattered. Gavin Stamp wrote about Lutyens in the *Architectural Review* as if he were engaged in a messianic mission of national, cultural and architectural salvation.

Some sense of how out of proportion the rhetoric had become can be judged by looking at the claim that Lutyens' self-evident genius had been censored for ideological reasons by something amounting to a leftist conspiracy. The absence of his name – and those of Nesfield, George, Newton, Lanchester, Baker, Blomfield, Dawber, Blow, and very many others – from Pevsner's *An Outline of European Architecture* has to be seen alongside the fact that it was Pevsner who was largely responsible for first bringing precisely these architects to the public's attention in his other writings, and that in the course of a 450-page summary of two thousand years of European architecture, much bigger omissions had been made – the whole of Italian Gothic architecture, of sixteenth-century Germany, and of Scandinavia for example – for which Pevsner himself apologised in his Introduction.

Not only were the committee hawks misrepresenting their enemies; they were misrepresenting their friends. Contemporaries of Lutyens had been far more balanced in their appreciation of him. H. S. Goodhart-Rendel, claimed by dilettantes from Kenneth Clark to John Betjeman as 'the father of us all', regarded Lutyens as a powerful talent but sometimes over-rated – in his design for the Cenotaph, for example. The *Architectural Review* was far more critical, failing to publish him at all as if he were somehow outside the realm of respectable architecture. But this was long before the progressive movement which the *AR* represented had become internationalised or Germanised or in any other sense unacceptable to the English. Its editor was resident architect to St Paul's Cathedral. He was hardly going to be a threat to the national interest.

The exhibition of Lutyens' work closed in early 1982, but its influence has persisted and the country houses which he and his contemporaries designed are enjoying an Indian summer among both architects and the public. As an example of how tastes have changed, the Georgian Group – a pressure group for the conservation of eighteenth-century architecture – has recently adapted its constitution in order to embrace twentith-century *neo*-Georgian architecture – buildings which even Roderick Gradidge has described as stilted and prim. In a sense, both sides have suffered from the sentimentality of the Lutyens campaign.

The story of Lutyens' re-emergence is a remarkable example of how a reputation can be misused when some ulterior purpose is at work. Lutyens was indeed an architect of invention. But in choosing him to be a figurehead for the promotion of conservatism in architecture, some of his more attractive features have had to be played down. A more honest picture of him presents him as far more interesting than the portrayal of him by his most enthusiastic advocates suggest.

Lutyens was undoubtedly one of this country's most successful architects – a man of enormous output and energy. Principally a domestic architect, he had built or enlarged two hundred country houses by the time he was thirty-five, an age when many architects today are just finishing off their first commissions. He went on to build the Viceroy's Palace in New Delhi when the British government decided to move the Indian capital from Calcutta, and this building triggered several other projects – all unbuilt – for new palaces from local maharajahs. He also built a large number of war memorials of which the most notable were the Cenotaph in London and Thiepval in France. There was at the same time a near total absence in his repertoire of offices and commercial buildings. Lutyens can be seen, therefore, as an architect who celebrated Empire: an architect of hearth and home, and of national grief.

To speak of him as a man of the Establishment, however, would be misleading. Although he had married up into the Lytton family, he never really adapted to the conventions expected of him. At Knebworth over Christmas he teased his niece, Lady Hermione Cobbold, telling her that he would pull all the hairpins out of her aunt's hair. At the childhood birthday parties of the Hon. Mrs Arthur Pollen, he would gallop round the room high-kicking like a chorus girl, after having put in a twelve-hour day at the office.

'He drew us pictures,' Mrs Pollen remembers, 'and he had a special way of tucking us up in bed which was known as the Uncle Ned tuck-up – and we loved him dearly, with his beaming face and big spectacles. Some bit of him, I think, didn't grow up. When the Aga Khan was there, he used to say: "Curtsey, curtsey, curtsey, here comes God!" Great fun, but that continual bubbling mirth and teasing can be a little shy-making when you're in your teens.'

His immediate family found his unrelenting pranks equally stressful to put up with for any length of time. 'He was very inarticulate,' says his daughter Mary Links, 'and he could only really express himself through either hugging you or drawing pictures for you. So we never had any conversation. I felt once when we were in Delhi together that I ought to make an effort to get to know him and talk to him about something that interested him. I think I was fifteen. And so I said to him "What are the essentials for becoming an architect?" And he didn't take his pipe out of his mouth or stop playing patience. He just said "All you have to know is that water runs downhill." I felt terribly snubbed.

'He embarrassed a young man in Delhi called Weston. He was sitting at our blackboard table and Father suddenly said to him "Are you any relation to the Great Western?" and he said "I'm not sure, sir." And everybody laughed, and the poor young man went red to the ears and I felt very sorry for him. He didn't mean to be unkind, I'm sure. He just couldn't resist it. I mean, he always said, whenever the butter came, "Butter late than never." And then in India, whenever he went out with his solar topi, he used to say "Topi or not topi?" And my mother used to get very bored with his puns, and say "Not that again, Neddy."'

Schoolboy jokes were Lutyens' invariable method of communication, and he was too shy or too insensitive to know what effect they could have. Behind them lay a vulnerable man, ill-equipped for the adult world. In company he could be boorish; at home, withdrawn. Emotionally he was immature and mawkish. He never dared go to the theatre because he cried easily. If he did entertain grand thoughts, they were never spoken of. He could neither respond to the intellectual demands of his daughter Elisabeth, the composer, nor the spiritual demands of his wife, Lady Emily Lytton, who, as their marriage went on, denied him her bed and became instead a follower of Krishnamurti and the cult of theosophy.

Lutyens responded to his business and marital frustrations by retreating into himself, which meant crossword puzzles, endless games of patience, and incessant tiny pipes of tobacco. At some times he would apologise unremittingly for his failings as a father and a husband; at others he would resort to flippancy to help him through a busy but anxious career made worse by perpetual 'money wowwies' – he could never pronounce his Rs – and tax arrears.

That he was given the opportunity to build homes and monuments for the good and the great is very much a measure of their patience. For his part, he never dignified his dealings with them. One hot day in India, during protracted discussions with government officials over a name for the new capital, he suggested 'Oozipore', and showed his boredom for the whole proceedings by pretending to fall asleep and letting his elbow slip repeatedly and noisily off the table.

Where other architects were formal, however, Lutyens used innocent charm. After offending the Vicereine Lady Hardinge and being sent to his room in disgrace as if he were a child, he wrote an apologetic note, which read: 'I bathe your feet with my tears and dry them with my hair; it is true that I have very little hair but then you have very little feet!' It was irresistible and he was forgiven at once.

To deal at length with Lutyens the man is amusing, but it is also the key to Lutyens the architect. His thought process was not so much large as various – *in*genious rather than genius. He made, for example, repeated visits to Delhi on the P&O line, and on each of his many letters to his five children he would embellish the company monogram in a different way, turning it into a tiger or a ballet dancer or a Chinaman. These visual puns, like his verbal puns, played on external appearances at the expense of meaning. The same was true of his architecture. The pilasters on his Midland Bank have already been referred to. At Nashdom, a large house he designed for entertaining and Ascot racing parties, he deflated the pretensions of his client with a simple whitewashed brick exterior. At Ilkley, he managed to install a black marble staircase against the wishes of his client on the grounds that when the client had made his wishes for an oak staircase known, Lutyens had said he thought that that was a pity and not received a further countermand.

This naughtiness is typical, as if Lutyens' buildings were gags from *Boy's Own Weekly*. But there is also a sweetness about them. In one of his houses, he designed a circular nursery which he said was to stop Nanny from standing the children in corners. His design for the new British Embassy in Washington included a nursery window which looked down over the hall where the guests arrived so that the ambassador's children could watch the social events from afar and not be completely excluded from the fun.

The homeliness of Lutyens' grander buildings had its roots in his childhood experience. He did not attend public school and seems not to have acquired the manners or the prejudices of a middle-class Victorian education. Instead, he was brought up by his sisters' governesses in the quiet Surrey village of Thursley, which left him ill-equipped for the formalities of social life and unable to compete in conventional ways with men. He also seems to have been happier in the company of women, children and – in India – servants. Herbert Ward, who worked as Lutyens' assistant in Delhi, remembers the relationship he had with his bearer, Pasotum. 'The bearer used to dress you in the morning. You'd hold out a foot and he'd put your sock on. But every time Pasotum put a sock on, Lutyens would push him over backwards with the other foot, never moving a muscle in his face. There was a wonderful relationship there. There were about fifteen winters that Lutyens spent going out to India and he always had the same bearer. When he finally left, Lutyens described the scene. "It was simply dreadful," he said. "Pasotum lifted up his head and howled like a wolf, and we both burst into tears!" '

Lutyens' interest in architecture was kindled by two women – Barbara Webb, a friend of his parents, and Gertrude Jekyll, the celebrated gardener who brought him as close as he would get to the Arts and Crafts movement. Together they travelled around the Surrey lanes in her dog-cart, making notes on rustic cottages and hedgerow plants. Once Lutyens came to practise architecture, however, he seems not to have enjoyed the studied naturalness of Miss Jekyll's gardens as much as his own more geometrical garden layouts, though she was often brought in to soften them with her planting. It was as if in Lutyens' gardens, the definition of the house extended beyond its walls into lawns that were rooms and paths that were corridors.

He seems to have been happiest, nevertheless, in his early cottage-style houses with their big gabled roofs and massive chimneys – features which his American contemporary Frank Lloyd Wright particularly admired him for. His more sober buildings – his Georgian town houses and his more opulent interiors – were often lifeless and dull, and according to Peter Inskip, they have got more so. 'They were originally decorated as whitewashed buildings, and then perhaps the entrance hall would be painted black with a white cornice, but very very simple. The buildings were also furnished with early eighteenth-century rush-seated ladderback chairs, perhaps bleached and scrubbed in a very primitive way. And one had a wonderful contrast between a rather grand house and peasanty furniture with rush-matting or, at Lindisfarne, oak floors painted white and dragged with duck-egg blue. When you go and see the houses today, there's wall-to-wall carpeting and comfortable three-piece suites which certainly don't go with Lutyens' intentions.'

Lutyens quickly outgrew the Surrey cottage style and launched himself into an exploration of other styles which was at first quite anarchic. In 1898, at the age of thirty, he built Le Bois des Moutiers for Guillaume Mallet in the small village of Varengeville outside Dieppe. The house rejoices in Tudor arches, Japanese windows, Elizabethan linenfold doors, a baronial fireplace, grid-paned windows, and a façade with a mouth, a nose and two eyes that looks like a Medusa's head. 'It was,' says Guillaume's grandson Robert Mallet, 'a catalogue of everything that he could do.' In addition it clearly showed his humour and his irreverence. But in its desperate search for the picturesque it posed problems about how he could proceed further. The limitation of the decorative eclecticism at Le Bois des Moutiers was that the more styles he collated, the less they fused into an artistic whole.

Several of his houses were ostensibly no more than exercises in stylistic composition and technique. They showed an immense facility with Baronial, Elizabethan, Queen Anne, and Palladian architecture, and a particular fondness for Christopher Wren, which led Lutyens to design in a style he described as his 'Wren-naissance'. In Lutyens' hands, however, these exercises went beyond imitation into a personal exploration of the ambiguities of historical authenticity. Homewood, his mother-in-law's house on the Knebworth estate, resembles a sixteenth-century weather-boarded cottage supposedly 'improved' two hundred years later by being given a classical porch and a pair of wings in the Tuscan style. In this way, he was providing the building with a fanciful four-hundred-year history, instead of limiting it to a single moment in time.

Authenticity was also challenged at Marsh Court in Hampshire where he undermined, and thereby showed his distance from, the strict morality of William Morris and the Arts and Crafts movement. Morris had founded the Society for the Protection of Ancient Buildings in an attempt to prevent medieval buildings from being restored to some fashionable notion of what they might originally have been like. The SPAB believed that repairs should be carried out without disguising the true age and history of the building and they highlighted those places where stonework needed replacing by repairing them with slips of red tile. At Marsh Court, Lutyens used the same technique for the sake not of truth but of falsification. He designed what purported to be a converted Tudor mansion that had apparently been repaired with tile and flint. He then used the same two materials for a chequer-board motif that ran round the walls like a dado – an architectural punchline that showed he was pulling your leg.

This game of historical collage required each stylistic element to retain its own identity. Creating a new blend of styles that turned the past into a vague generalisation was not what Lutyens was interested in. Many of his fellow architects felt differently, especially his rival and former friend Herbert Baker, with whom he sat on the planning committee for New Delhi some years later. Baker wanted the new administrative capital to be a symbolic synthesis between English and Indian architecture, an approach that Lutyens felt he had grown out of long before. In 1919, when he came across Baker's work in South Africa, he clucked and tutted. It was 'full of schoolboy errors – a sort of early Me', he said.

Six empires had conquered India over the centuries and each had stamped its architectural footprints on the country. Lutyens felt therefore that Indian architecture was always too corrupt to be worthy of imitation. He especially disliked its Muslim features, believing that its domes and minarets were cramped, and that its pointed arches were imperfect because, unlike round arches, their proportions could be stretched to fit any space. But his dislike was even greater because it was so favoured by the Viceroy Lord Hardinge, and his committee, whom Lutyens regarded as stuffed shirts unworthy of his time and attention. Seated on elephants and horses, they would ride out on what he regarded as tedious expeditions, searching for old buildings that might provide them with the model they were looking for, when to Lutyens, the answer was simply to entrust *him* with the design.

Unable to compromise on any point, Lutyens threatened to resign when he could not get his own way. 'Can't you play cricket?' Baker inquired. He could not; his game was solitaire.[1] Finally the workload, instead of being pooled, was sectioned off and Lutyens was entrusted with the design of the Viceroy's palace. This he completed in a style regarded by the historian Narayani Gupta, who specialises in the years of the British Raj, as essentially Roman Baroque – St Peter's with a few Mogul trimmings.

Style was only one aspect of Lutyens' thinking at New Delhi. Just as his best exteriors are those which offer a sequence of architectural periods, so his best plans are those which stress a sequence of physical movements. In his country houses, for example, his

---

[1] 'Any talent I may have,' Lutyens once told Osbert Sitwell, 'was due to a long illness as a boy, which afforded me time to think . . . because I was not allowed to play games, and so had to teach myself . . . to use my eyes instead of my feet.'

corridors and staircases are often the most entertaining places to be in, and here he would exaggerate their length and the details of construction without regard to cost.

He did the same at Delhi, creating a two-mile-long boulevard which swept past Baker's two secretariats, on either side, without a second glance. The climax of the route was intended to be the Viceroy's palace, but events – as is now well known – worked out differently. The site had a partial slope to it, so that the boulevard rose slowly but then levelled out halfway up, making the palace appear to sink into the ground when approached from a distance. Lutyens argued – prophetically as it turned out – that this would be fatal for India and that the Indians would see it as a portent. He pleaded with Baker to replan the secretariats so that the slope could be altered, but Baker refused. Lutyens regarded it as the defeat of his career, calling it his Bakerloo. 'What a pity it is that Baker's alphabet doesn't begin with A for Architecture instead of B for Baker,' he said.

Such experiences encouraged Lutyens to look for a new direction in architecture – a purer language in which to express his unique mastery of the craft. He came to feel that his subject matter was really geometry, for it was in geometry that he could demonstrate the greater ingenuity of his mind. Some years later, in 1933, the architectural historian Sir John Summerson saw a demonstration of this. It was at his dining club, the Whitefriars, and Lutyens was guest of honour. Summerson had made what he now describes as an impertinent speech, accusing Lutyens of not being modern enough.

Lutyens' reply was unexpected. 'He picked up an apple,' Sir John recalls, 'and he sliced it in a crooked sort of way so that it fell apart in two or more pieces which then fitted together in a most beautiful and geometrical clinch. And I remember so well his obvious pleasure in doing it; and there you have something absolutely central to Lutyens – not so much in the country houses but in the later work like the vast Memorial to the Missing at Thiepval in northern France. At first sight, you might think it to be almost pure solid geometry – a triumphal arch converted into a mass of cubes and rectangles. When you come to look at it closely, it's very much more than that; it's like one triumphal arch crossing the tracks of another, combining into a complete and indivisible geometrical whole, just like the apple that he cut at the dinner at the Whitefriars.'

Lutyens' fascination with geometry seemed to take architectural decisions out of the realm of argument. John Brandon-Jones, who now runs the architectural practice started by C. F. A. Voysey, recalls him being asked at a students' evening at the Architectural Association why he dimensioned his drawings in sixty-fourths of an inch, since no builder would ever work that accurately, and Lutyens replying that if he dimensioned his buildings in round inches, people would think that the nearest inch was good enough, while if he dimensioned his buildings in sixty-fourths he might just get them to the nearest eighth.

Lutyens found truth in precision. His favourite roof pitch was 54.45 degrees – the diagonal of a rectangle with sides in the proportion of 1 to the square root of 2. Roof surfaces at right angles to each other and pitched at this incline share a perfect 45-degree hip. He was also fascinated to discover from his daughter Elisabeth that just as architecture was based on the Greek orders, so music was based on Greek modes, which in turn were expressions of an underlying geometrical relationship.

Geometry also helped in the design of his few commercial buildings in the City of London where it was becoming increasingly difficult to transpose classical architecture onto façades higher than five floors. But it was the Cenotaph, the design which made him a household name, where his geometrical perambulations were most extensive and most introverted. He had been asked by the government to design a wooden catafalque that could be used as a saluting point for the first Armistice parade in 1919, and he remembered an Italian stone bench he had seen in Gertrude Jekyll's garden thirty years earlier. It stood at one end of a broad avenue and E. V. Lucas, the editor of *Punch*, had defined it as a 'cenotaph' – an empty tomb.

Lutyens' adaptation of this design captured the mood of the time in a remarkable way, without either making death heroic by resorting to statues of fallen soldiers, or denominational by resorting to crucifixes. Just as he was able, later, to persuade the Imperial War Graves Commission, against the advice of Herbert Baker, to adopt plain, rectangular headstones for the battlefield cemeteries in France, so in Whitehall he was able to focus the nation's mourning on an impersonal symbol. The Cenotaph was based on Miss Jekyll's bench, but in Lutyens' mind it was a composition of pure geometry, the calculations for which took thirty-three pages of notes. The verticals in the design were angled to meet 900 feet overhead, while all the horizontal surfaces were segments of circles with a common radius 900 feet below ground. This may well have been what Baker had in mind in his obituary of Lutyens in *The Times* in 1944 when he wrote that 'he

concentrated his extraordinary powers on the abstract and intellectual values to the sacrifice sometimes, I considered, of human
and national sentiment.'

The design which Lutyens was never able to complete would
have been the culmination of his thinking at Whitehall and Thiepval. It was for a Roman Catholic cathedral in Liverpool so vast and
intricate that it would have looked a little like a Turkish hillside
village. It is perhaps surprising that he should have won the
commission, considering the number of perfectly qualified Catholic architects available. In addition, the only religious influence
on his life were his wife and the young Jiddu Krishnamurti, the
boy leader of the Theosophical movement and a frequent house
guest. Both were deeply opposed to established religions.
'Lutyens used to say he was glad I didn't read religious books,'
says Krishnamurti today; 'I was more likely to say something
original.' Herbert Ward also remembers that he would skate off
the subject if he ever tried to tackle him on religion. 'If he'd lost
something, he'd search around for it, saying "Oh God, where did
I put my pencil, oh God, where's my pencil, oh God. . . . Oh here
it is. Thank you God!"'

More important, perhaps, was the fact that Liverpool was going
to be the crowning achievement of all those elements of architecture he had had to learn, rather than those he picked up naturally,
for geometry was a discipline he had had to struggle with. Lutyens
was by nature an instinctive designer. According to John
Brandon-Jones, he had an entirely picturesque attitude to everything he did, even if it was a classical design. 'The tendency was to
make it *look* right. He didn't want to show the rainwater pipes on
the front, for example, so he took them down the inside of the
building. Or he designed long gutters in wood with lead linings
which didn't hold water. He took terrible risks which Philip Webb
or Voysey or even Norman Shaw would never have taken, which is
why a Lutyens house is much heavier on maintenance than the
average building ought to be.

'I think he looked at the Surrey cottages in the way John Sell
Cotman looked at them, absorbing an awful lot about massing and
composition and clumping chimneys together, but I don't think he
worried about how the thing was made to stand up. He made
rough sketches and then at a later stage he laid his set square over
and calculated the diagonals and checked the shape of the window
panes. He was absolutely an intuitive architect who then tried to
impose a certain order on things.'

Herbert Ward agrees. 'He'd been absorbed by the Parthenon

and the way the steps are all curved, and the columns lean in, and the outer columns are thicker, and he felt that this was done by eye and then the calculations came afterwards – that the Greeks looked at each thing they did and if they weren't satisfied they had it altered until it did look right. And when it was finished, then they could work out mathematically how it was done.'

It has been easy for enthusiasts of traditional architecture to use Lutyens as their model. On his last visit to London in 1981, the American architect Philip Johnson harangued his English counterparts at the RIBA for being so unsure of themselves that they had to look abroad to Le Corbusier and Mies van der Rohe for their heroes; didn't they realise that in Edwin Lutyens they had the most original designer of the twentieth century standing on their very doorstep?

But is Lutyens a good model? Though he received endless praise during the course of his career, he was always embarrassed by it. He believed that architecture could no more be spoken about than drawing could be taught. At the presentation ceremony for his King's Gold Medal in 1921 he was emotional but curt: 'What we want is deeds, not words,' he said, and sat down. Unlike Herbert Baker, who always carried a book of poetry in his pocket, Lutyens had no use for rhetoric. He refused to check the galley proofs of Weaver's *Country Life* book and was stubborn and intractable about giving him even basic information. He found his son Robert's analysis of his work ('The Armature of Planes') baffling. Lectures and after-dinner speeches terrified him.

In architecture, too, while Baker made constant sketches of attractive details that caught his eye, Lutyens tended to rely on memory alone. His European sketchbooks are mostly records of what he disliked. His office drawings were regarded as nothing more than letters to the builder and never the works of art that his draughtsmen tried to make them. And in spite of the liberties and mannerisms of his work, he was puritanical about design, refusing to offer himself as an examplar, and insisting always that good design should arise from first principles.

He might nevertheless have been amused that the stuffed shirts whom he so disliked and who found him so boorish are now his greatest fans, for they have so little in common. He was never a dilettante, nor would he have been able to understand the preciousness with which his work is now greeted. Although he thought that modern architecture was haphazard and crude, he admired the adventurous spirit of its young practitioners. His own work shows a steady rejection of the sentimental in favour of the systematic organisation which can be seen in his modular design for Liverpool. He disliked pomposity and formality of every kind; he thrived in situations where he could celebrate the humorous, the informal and the utilitarian. As Elisabeth Lutyens has said: 'Father was not patriotic about Empire. He liked the idea of anything English, and though he was anything but an intellectual snob, he did like peers and kings and queens, which I thought was nice, simple snobbery. I don't think he did Delhi to the glory of the Empire; it was a wonderful opportunity for an architect.'

Lutyens did not want to be a national monument, nor did he like to gas about himself, except in his own curious way. Sailing to Delhi during the Great War, he put a note in his inflatable waistcoat which read: 'If my lifeless body should be picked up, would the finder please return this waistcoat to my family without undoing the stopper. I should like them to enjoy my last breath.' He envisaged the family sitting solemnly around the dining-room table while their solicitor, with great ceremony, pulled out the stopper and announced as the air hissed away: 'Your father's last breath.'

It should be a lesson to anyone who tries to blow up his memory that Lutyens was a deflater to the last.

The Reversible Mackintosh

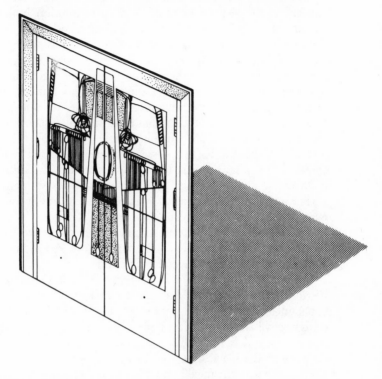

Glasgow of the 1890s was a city of shipyards, heavy industry and finance institutions. Its heavy commercial buildings malingered under a layer of atmospheric grime and a perpetually sulphurous sky. In many ways similar to Chicago, the second city of America, Glasgow could boast that it was the second city of an entire Empire – a boast to which its various business enterprises all lent their accumulated weight.

Yet Glasgow was home to a most un-Glaswegian aestheticism in the arts – a movement more extreme, more advanced, and in many ways more creative than its counterparts in London and Europe. Glasgow painters were being recognised with some astonishment at home and abroad as constituting a significant new school, and in 1898, two of them – John Lavery and E. A. Walton – were made corresponding members of the Vienna Sezession. But aestheticism touched architecture and the applied arts as well. In both these the leading exponent was Charles Rennie Mackintosh.

Mackintosh brought a delicacy to Glasgow which contradicted

everything the city then stood for. He introduced whiteness and lightness into designs that were conspicuously lacking in substance, and he paid the price for his presumption, both before and after his death in 1928, by being neglected and rejected. When the furniture which he had designed for the Glasgow School of Art and Glasgow's Cranston Tearooms went out of style, much of it was consigned to junk heaps and the Corporation tip. In the 1940s, the acting director of the Glasgow School of Art opposed efforts by Thomas Howarth, a member of staff and subsequently Mackintosh's biographer, to commemorate his association with the art school in an exhibition. The partners in Keppie Henderson – Mackintosh's former firm – were equally belligerent: Henderson out of professional jealousy, Keppie because Mackintosh had been engaged to, and then jilted, his sister Jessie many years earlier – the memory of which was reputed still to prompt tears even in her old age. As a result, his name was effectively censored by those who had been closest to him. There was no reference to him, for example, in the prospectus of the Art School until 1960–61, which sounds inconceivable today.

Former friends were of little help. William Davidson, who became the trustee of the Mackintosh estate after his death, was so appalled at Mackintosh's treatment at the hands of the most upright city institutions that he refused to release any of the items in his possession for public scrutiny. 'On one occasion, I had dinner with the Davidsons,' recalls Professor Howarth, 'and during the course of the meal I said that one of the problems I had was that I hadn't been able to find any Mackintosh correspondence. So after dinner, he brought out a pile of letters tied up in a blue ribbon. And I said: "May I take these home with me to study or would you prefer me to read them here?" And he said: "Oh, you can't read those, those are private letters!"'

Far from safeguarding his memory, such protectiveness helped to prevent Mackintosh from reaching a wider public. This in turn made his work more vulnerable after the war. With ringroads being driven through the old tenement districts of Glasgow and the population relocated, his schools and churches were left stripped of the communities they had once served, and at risk of demolition. At best, they could be saved for new uses – uses to which the vagaries of local authority by-laws made them stubbornly unsuited.

Leonard Turpie is a lawyer and former councillor who sat on the City's planning committee in the 1960s. 'Mackintosh was a planner's nightmare,' he remembers. 'It was one of those tragicomedies where you couldn't live with him and you couldn't live without him. Rehousing was underway, the motorways were underway, and what one spent most of one's time doing was trying to make the most constructive and the least destructive decisions. Take the Scotland Street School, for example. We thought at one time of dismantling it stone by stone and re-erecting it somewhere else. But the Scottish Education Authority said: No, it will not comply with modern regulations for schools. I remember the Ingram Street Tearooms. We went down there – someone was trying to make a go of it on a commercial basis. They'd put Mackintosh tartan carpets down – *hideous* along with the bleached lime and pale colours of Charles Rennie Mackintosh.[1] We thought of restoring it as a tearoom and the Fire Inspector said it wouldn't match the fire regulations. Environmental Health said it wouldn't do at all. I tell you, after they'd turned down one project after another, I said to the officials who were with me: "Is it all right if I use the urinal?" And one of them said solemnly: "That's against the law!" For abstruse environmental health reasons, I couldn't even use the wretched urinal!'

Mackintosh's unpopularity suggests that even at his height he was only a phenomenon of fashion. He saw success abroad and notoriety at home collapse into oblivion everywhere. He had created a style, was stereotyped by it, and left stranded when he and the public failed to agree on what should come next. In some ways it was a personal tragedy, but he was also the victim of larger events going on in Europe which with the birth of the Bauhaus in Germany were to make the whole of British art seem redundant.

The style which brought Mackintosh to prominence came not from the architectural language in which he was trained but from the nest of artists in Tite Street, Chelsea. From them he developed a recognisably *art nouveau* technique, just ahead of its appearance on the Continent and ahead, too, of the first publication of the *Studio* in 1893. In manner it was floral, abstract and elongated; in mood it was obsessive and inconsequential, like a doodle, and Mackintosh learned to deliver it with increasing economy until he had turned the whole art of composition into a question of exaggeration. It enabled all claims on his skill to be answered two-dimensionally, no matter how much – like furniture and interiors – they called for three-dimensional treatment. Which is why his chairs cannot be sat in without discomfort or without risk to the spine and why they have a tendency to collapse.

[1]Mackintosh never used tartan.

In his aestheticism, Mackintosh was rather like the frog in the fable, allowing the twentieth century to ride on his back, only to be stung in mid-current for his troubles. What he swam between was Victoriana, which *separated* art from everything else, and Modernism, which *identified* art with everything else. Art for Art's Sake did not know there *was* anything else, as the art historian Peter Vergo demonstrated in his exhibition *Vienna 1900* at the 1983 Edinburgh Festival.

'This was a period,' says Vergo, 'when the traditional definitions – architect, cabinet-maker, designer – are breaking down, and the architect becomes a maestro figure who wants to orchestrate the whole composition. He sees the house as an interior as well as an exterior. He wants to do the furnishings, the décor, the cutlery, the jewellery worn by the lady of the house. The Germans sometimes refer to this as *Gesamtkunstwerk*, the "total work of art", taking the term from Wagner, and it does give some sense of what they were trying to do.

'After all, one of the characteristics of late nineteenth-century Symbolist art is the idea that art permeates life – it's not just something you do on a Sunday afternoon when you go to an art gallery, but something which regulates your life. I think the designers simply took up this essentially Symbolist notion, translated it into physical reality in their designs, and found for a short time patrons who were prepared to go along with it and pay for it. But it was a very short-lived phenomenon.'

This element of other-worldliness was welcomed in Europe, and especially in the Austria of Mahler, Klimt and Freud. As a participant in the Eighth Sezession Exhibition in Vienna in 1900, Mackintosh is said to have been drawn through the streets in a flower-bedecked carriage by local art students. His work in the exhibition was described by one Austrian critic as *mystic* and *ascetic*, 'not in a Christian sense, but with the scent of heliotrope, with well-manicured hands, and a delicate sensuousness'. Even Mackintosh's cupboards, he said, were straight, white, and serious-looking, like young girls going to their first Holy Communion.

They weren't having any of this kind of thing in Kelvinside, the Glasgow suburb where Mackintosh lived. He was already a little suspect in his serge jackets and floppy bows, and his wife Margaret MacDonald (no children, mind) was probably no better than she should be. Her own designs, and those of her sister Frances, had appeared alongside Aubrey Beardsley's in a volume of *The Yellow Book* in 1896, the book Oscar Wilde was carrying when they came for him at the Cadogan Hotel, and that was enough to taint them both for life.

Mackintosh had other handicaps. He had a brooding temper and a quick tongue which he used with increasing frequency on clients and office staff who irritated him. But he was also handicapped by his facility. He could do all the things that qualified him for the title 'Artist' in the Symbolist dictionary. He designed buildings, furniture, cutlery, murals, stained glass, metalwork, doorknobs and light fittings, as well as posters, line drawings, water-colours and gesso panels. But that range of talents which would be death to hide anywhere else was a liability in Britain, where he was regarded as too arty to be a craftsman and too crafty to be an artist.

On top of that, he started off his career being just too fashionable to be taken seriously. The *Architectural Review*, launched in London in 1896, remained quite stubbornly unaware – on paper, at least – of his existence throughout his working years, as it had been of Lutyens. In 1906 the *Builder's Journal* was still capable of saying only that Mackintosh's buildings were 'characteristic of their architect' and that the photographs spoke for themselves.

The artistic intensity of Mackintosh's work ensured that any attention he received would come from the art world rather than the architectural community. Yet when an obviously enthusiastic Gleeson White, editor of the *Studio*, gave the Mackintosh group its first lengthy review in 1897, he had to struggle for words. He conceded that their work was in opposition to the neo-Gothic orthodoxy of the day, that it lacked a proper archaeological basis, and that it was too eccentric and personal either to be recommended for imitation or assessed fairly by critics. In mitigation, he could only suggest that it was new, and different, and that it was too early to say what would become of it. In other words, in replying to attacks that were already in the air, Gleeson White was far more fluent in voicing the disapproval he was trying to argue against than in expressing what it was that had excited him.

Why was Mackintosh's work so difficult to come to terms with? It may be that it never had the stamina to make the transition from marginal scribbles in a notebook to a fully-fledged artistic style. Its first manifestation came not in his architectural work, which consisted of conventional essays in Gothic and classical design, but in drawings and illustrations carried out in an ethereal, melancholic style, heavily indebted to Pre-Raphaelitism, Beardsley, Toorop and Rossetti – drawings with an exaggerated interest in repetition, especially the repetition of lyrically organic lines. It was a style he shared with Herbert McNair, a fellow draughtsman in the office where he worked, and with the two MacDonald sisters, whom they had met as fellow students at the Glasgow School of Art. At a time of female emancipation, this pooling of resources by 'The Four', as they called themselves, reflected badly on the men. Even in the 1930s, the *Architectural Review*, which by now had discovered Mackintosh through his death, was still putting it about that he had been held back by his wife. Yet Mackintosh had said of her: 'Margaret has genius; I have only talent.'

The man who brought Mackintosh and Margaret together was their principal at art school, Francis Newbery. His daughter, the flower painter Mary Newbery-Sturrock, kept in touch with Mackintosh in his later life, and watched him one day at work.[1] 'Artists usually use soft, silky 3B or 4B pencils but architects use hard pencils – F or H – and Mackintosh was doing these slight wiry designs with such a marvellous line – completely controlled and completely clean. Somebody said that Mrs Mackintosh was the great genius, she was the great influence, she was this, she was that. And I said how could somebody who worked with 3B, 4B, 6B pencils and very woolly water-colours, as she did, influence somebody who worked with F and H pencils and a hard line such as she could never possibly have drawn except after years and years of training?'

The controversy about Mackintosh was enough to defeat him in his own lifetime. As a young man, he had thought of himself as the scourge of the Philistines, a David fighting the forces of artistic ignorance and indifference. By the age of forty, however, the battle was already lost. Even in Austria, interest in him as an exotic, offshore phenomenon was giving way to an interest in a more conventional and florid homegrown aesthetic. In response to rejection from all quarters, Mackintosh took to the bottle, and then to his feet. His last fourteen years were spent in virtual exile in Suffolk, Chelsea and the Pyrenees, where he gave up doing textile and furniture designs in favour of water-colours of coastal and mountain scenes broken down into neurotically reiterated fragments of colour.

The arguments about Mackintosh have continued to rumble on without him. In the light of the blurring of artistic identities which

---

[1]This was a commission from Mackintosh's patron, W. J. Bassett-Lowke, who owned an engineering and model-making firm, and for whom he designed furniture, architectural alterations and graphic display work, including this job – trade stamps for the backs of business envelopes.

Peter Vergo pointed to as a characteristic of the turn of the century, Mackintosh's very identity has tended to be in dispute. Was he an artist or an architect? An architect or a designer? A designer or a decorator? And was he a man of the nineteenth or the twentieth century? A pioneer of Modernism or a late Victorian? To the extent that these questions ask us to think about the terms they use, they are useful; to the extent that they create artificial alternatives, they are not.

Recently, however, Mackintosh has acquired a role which puts all questions about the quality and status of his work into the background. He has been elected, by almost unanimous consent, the Flavour of the Decade. He has been hailed the hero of Glasgow. His furniture is sold in expensive facsimile editions throughout the world by manufacturers in Italy, Spain and Japan.[1] Originals sell at auction for giddy prices. His few remaining buildings are on every Clydeside tourist itinerary. And Glasgow tills ring to the sale of souvenir mugs, oven gloves and T-shirts. Only the brave and the foolhardy dare recall that it was not always thus. What has happened?

Mackintosh grew up at a time when young architects who would have been satisfied with a Grand Tour of Europe 50 years earlier were beginning to go off on Modest Tours of England as well. The reasons were the same: to observe at first hand the architecture which they would be incorporating into their work for the rest of their careers.

Mackintosh was no exception, taking himself on walking tours not just of Italy but of southern England and returning home with obligatory notebooks filled with sketches of half-timbered cottages, moss-encrusted roof-tiles, clapboarded fascias, and thatched roofs. Olde Englande was being pursued with almost religious fervour by the most progressive architects of the day, and Mackintosh allied himself with it in two ways: by associating himself with the aims of the English Arts and Crafts movement, and by searching for an equivalent revival of a distinct architectural identity for Scotland.

He illustrated his commitment to the first of these in a lecture to a Glasgow literary society in about 1905. 'The Alhambra,' he said, 'gorgeous and refined, more beautiful perhaps than any other building, is yet of a lower kind of architecture than the far plainer but more enduring country churches of England or Normandy.'

---

[1]Professor Thomas Howarth is now bringing out a range of his own in Canada.

It is in these terms that he is viewed by Andy Macmillan, Professor at what is now the Mackintosh School of Art in Glasgow. 'Mackintosh's strength, and the reason why he is *the* figure to come out of the English House movement paradoxically [as a Scot] is that he remembered why Philip Webb and William Morris got into the business of vernacular architecture: that through devices like the bay window or the dormer in the roof or the lean-to extension, the needed space in the house could burst through the outside shell of the building, whereas under the Renaissance style, the external form was predetermined, and the space had to be disciplined to stay inside that predetermined form. So when our students use the bay window [in their designs], they're not necessarily just using a superficial device; they're recognising the principle that Mackintosh adduced, that the space can come through the shell if it needs to.'

Professor Macmillan's reading of Mackintosh as an Arts and Crafts man does not however jeopardise his reputation as a Scottish architect – or at least, a distinctly un-English one. 'Mackintosh's education he received in a school of art which certainly had international connections. His drawing would be learnt from Italian and French buildings. But his everyday experience of life was Scottish. We only have one building material – stone. We use it for walls, we use it for roofs, we sometimes roughcast it. So our buildings tend to be very simple, very prismatic, very austere compared to the wealth of building materials to be found in England. Mackintosh's first experience of the environment, therefore, is of austere buildings in a pretty majestic landscape, and a pretty big industrial town to give him the picture of what a town was like – a town very much more European than English. So to his perception of England he brought this basic Scottish background, and perhaps it was that background that allowed him to interpret the wealth of opportunity that English vernacular architecture offered.'

It is on the strength of this kind of interpretation that Mackintosh has become a rallying point for several causes – pre-Modern architecture, anti-Modern architecture, Romanticism, regionalism, Scottish nationalism, handicrafts, and tourism. But this only raises the question of whether he is the best vehicle for these various interests, or even an appropriate one.

An example of the dangers of regarding Mackintosh as an Arts and Crafts figure is given by Mary Newbery-Sturrock. 'I think the idea that he should always have been doing watercolours is a false idea. He was an architect or nothing. He really took to water-colours because he was never going to be idle but he was truly an architect. He never put a foot wrong with his little square bits of wrought iron. The bell on the stairs, the bird at the top of the School of Art – very few people could design such simple things so well. They really show a power, and it breaks my heart that it didn't get more use. Glasgow could have produced a Le Corbusier. It had a man of equal inventiveness and power and it just didn't use it. I think Nature very often uses a million seeds for a couple of plants; Mackintosh was one of the seeds that didn't germinate. He didn't fall on the right sort of soil.'

That is one interpretation. A rather different story comes from Juliet Kinchin, Senior Assistant Keeper with the Glasgow Museums, where she has special responsibility for the City's collection of original Mackintosh furniture. 'His craftsmanship was excruciating,' she says. 'He just wasn't interested in craft. He was a drawing-board designer, he was interested in the visuals, and I think one of the greatest mistakes is to associate him with the Arts and Crafts movement. Really, his ideas were anathema to artist-craftsmen. Having had to conserve various items of his furniture, I know the extent of the repairs we've had to make. For instance, the majority of his [ladderback] chairs have all had to have slats reinforcing the back. He could streamline these traditional forms and get rid of the raking, but it's that very raking which makes it a good sound design, and when you just have straight legs it puts incredible stress on the joints. His joints were very weak, with lots of glue and pretty cheap wood and nasty woodstains.'

Mackintosh's ability to build competently might seem an essential prerequisite of his reputation both as a late Arts and Crafts designer, and as a source of inspiration to the moderns who came after him. Yet worrying about whether a chair or a building stands up can be a pettifogging thing when compared with a designer's overall vision, and Mackintosh – like Walter Gropius, for example – can be thought of as having designed at a much higher level than mere structural competence. Indeed, he created an aesthetic which gave subsequent designers and craftsmen a goal to aim for, just as the Bauhaus was to do, even though the Bauhaus translated the dependence of technology on art into a dependence by art on technology.

The view of Mackintosh as part of an art-historical chain of inspiration, handing on his Promethean fire to the next generation, is how he was presented to art history by the historian Nikolaus Pevsner. Pevsner was the first to write about him at any length (in an essay in Italian in 1950), portraying him as one of the pioneers of modern design. But while there are similarities between his simplicity of form and the simplicity which architects of the 1930s strove for, not everyone nowadays accepts this reading of him as a prophet of the new.

'Windyhill, the house he designed for William Davidson in 1904, is picturesque but in a rather austere way,' says Dr Frank Walker of the Architecture Department at Strathclyde University. 'The reason for that is perhaps because of the choice of materials which are very simple. There is for example no stonework to be seen, there is no carving, all we're faced with is grey roughcast and blue-grey slates. So whereas in the work of [his contemporary Sir Robert] Lorimer one is distracted by – or entertained by – the texture of the stonework or the carving, in Mackintosh one is faced purely with form. He doesn't pay very close attention to the building construction details, for example, compared with Lorimer's work, and yet it's that very elimination of the detailing which seems to focus attention on the form. Maybe this relates to his own graphic beginnings – he's very much a designer architect rather than a builder architect.

'So it's probably something of a mistake to read into Mackintosh more Modernism than is there. Inevitably when Pevsner first wrote about him, and when Howarth wrote, things were seen from a Modernist point of view, and the relationships forward were the things which interested these writers, whereas later writers like Robert Macleod have a better historical view of him as the end of the Victorian era developing as far as it could go.'

Robert Macleod is a practising architect, and a former professor of architecture in Canada and at Bristol. His book on Mackintosh, to which Frank Walker refers, first came out in 1968, and the thesis which underlies it is two-fold. He argues that Mackintosh was not so much a theorist whose vision was fulfilled by the Bauhaus, as the fulfilment of an earlier theorist, the English architect William Lethaby – a man who never managed to fulfil his own ambitions. He also argues that in his craftsmanlike approach to his work, Mackintosh provides a role model for the architect of today. This simultaneous insistence on Mackintosh as both a primary and secondary figure ought to be self-cancelling: it certainly gets Macleod into arguments over other interpretations – even favourable interpretations of his own ideas, like Frank Walker's.

'Actually I don't mind,' says Macleod. 'I called Mackintosh in one sense at the end of my book one of the last of the Victorians.

But I was trying to counterbalance the traditional view of him as simply a pioneer of the Modern Movement who hadn't understood the Modern Movement yet.[1] That modernity [of the Modern Movement] was based on a self-conscious use of modern materials and what appeared to be modern forms, whereas the kind of pragmatic modernity that Mackintosh practised and that Lethaby preached was a modernity which was prepared to accept from whatever source the appropriate means to the end at that moment.'

The simplicity of Mackintosh's forms may have been exaggerated by the tight budgets he had to work under. His commissions tended to come less from wealthy business patrons than from lovers of 'advanced' art. It was an architecture, then, of functional expediency. But if that was solely the case, how does one explain the apparently tacked-on porch at Windyhill, the tacked-on staircase tower on the front façade, and the dormer windows in the roof, all of which come together in a riot of collision and misalignment which Mackintosh delightfully sets up and then refuses to resolve? Mannerisms as gauche as these are much more a self-conscious copying of quaint medieval clumsiness than the application of function dictating form. One *can* argue that they are pragmatic modernity, but not without a struggle. Architecture cannot be pragmatically modern *and* affectedly old-fashioned at the same time.

Peter Vergo believes that Mackintosh belongs to a different kind of architectural debate – one which has far more to do with the mysterious, atmospheric image-making in which the Mackintosh group first indulged, and for which they were dubbed the Spook School – though he does not typecast them in this role. 'I think Mackintosh came out of that at quite an early age,' he says. 'The Glasgow Spook School was very short-lived and more associated with Margaret MacDonald. By the early 1900s, they were moving away from that heaviness and clutter of the nineteenth century, away from the overblown and pompous, towards economy, lightness and severity. One sees this in the designs that Mackintosh did for Kate Cranston, this extraordinary character who had a succession of tearooms in Glasgow, and for whom Mackintosh did a range of interiors and furniture.

'For a period the Cranston designs became lighter and lighter and more functional – although, having said more functional, some of the furniture doesn't stand up very well to continuous use.

---

[1]Robert Macleod is referring to prewar attitudes to Mackintosh.

These very tall, high-backed chairs – these days very few people sit on them for fear of collapsing, but if you do sit on them, they're very uncomfortable, and I think the reason for this is a search for novelty. After all, things like chairs are functional forms that have developed over many centuries in terms of human anatomy, and there aren't many things you can do that are totally novel. Therefore, if you want to appear to be new and exciting and you start changing a design, you run the risk of defying ergonomics.'

Does that mean that the argument about Mackintosh is more properly conducted at the level of fashion?

'Very much so,' says Vergo. 'There was a quite distinct cultural and social group in Vienna and Germany. To some extent, it's the Jewish bourgeoisie. I think architects like Mackintosh were not appealing to the traditional upper classes at all, but they were appealing to very rich clients. For example, there's a set of Mackintosh competition designs done for a project called *The House of an Art Lover* in which there was an enormously elaborate music room which could have seated fifty or sixty people perhaps, with an organ, and very elaborate furnishings and décor. It was very much a matter of fashion, of going against aristocratic taste and people trying to outbid one another, keeping up with the Joneses, having the latest, the ultimate in furniture and interior design – very much a question of fashion.'

'That's perfectly true,' acknowledges Robert Macleod. 'I think that Mackintosh furniture exemplifies that lovely tension between the visual image on the one hand and the nature and purpose of the thing on the other. Mackintosh was extremely taken with the sheer seductiveness of the forms he was using. On the other hand, there is a functional base underlying it if you take the entire function into account, which in this case would involve costume and the way in which people use chairs and furniture. I've always been struck by Mackintosh's formal chairs on which all of society never sat anyway – they simply perched. And if an Edwardian woman sat in one, with a bustle back and an enormous hat, you could never lie back in that chair in any event; you were meant to be poised against it. And so his chairs represent a kind of functionalism that was not concerned with style *per se*.'

How then does Robert Macleod distinguish between function and the more ornamental aspects of design? 'Ferguson, the historian in the mid-nineteenth century, made a useful distinction between ornament that was constructed and construction that was ornamented. The latter – construction that was ornamented – was really the basis of the serious Gothic Revival and the Arts and

Crafts movement. Mackintosh had actually used that phrase in one of his lectures, and he often took constructive necessities and then used them as the springboard for some of the most fantastic visual solutions. I'm thinking, for example, of the basement of his School of Art, where with the most amazing ingenuity he's extended the T-beams and got the poor blacksmith with an acetylene torch to cut back the web and flanges for the whole depth, and then curl them into a series of roses for the purpose of retaining the beam above. This was a function which could have been performed by two simple lug screws in each one, but which in fact was satisfied by a different ornamental rose for every single beam along the length of the room. Now that still was construction that was ornamented, [although] it could be argued that it might be ornament that was constructed as well' – which leaves us with the problem that Mackintosh's work tends to defy even the most well-meaning claims made for it, including those of Mackintosh himself.

If there was no room to accommodate his work within the conventional architectural circles of his day in Scotland and England, there was equally no room to accommodate it within his own theories. By his plea for the stocky primitivism of English and Norman churches, and his insistence on the Alhambra's beauty as something inferior, he was implicitly criticising his own designs – or part of them. What roughcast, weather-beaten toughness there is in his buildings exists only on the exteriors of his buildings, and then only in his domestic work, or on the minor elevations of his public work. Behind the façade, the interiors have an insubstantial quality with their delicate pink and pastel colouring and their flat, stencilled wall motifs. They convey the sense that with the least breeze blowing through the translucent curtains that hang in the windows like pennants, the room will collapse. On that count alone, Mackintosh fails to satisfy fully his own Arts and Crafts criteria.

Evidence for Mackintosh's second stated concern – Scottishness – can be seen in his use of certain motifs that occur in medieval Scottish architecture: heavy, plain, harled, white-washed, bluewashed or greywashed walls; small, randomly-disposed *flèche* windows without cills; steep but unornamented gables; and wilfully clumsy service corridors and back stairs. But whether this really represented an attempt to remake Scottish architecture is doubtful considering Mackintosh's eclecticism. Not only did he take from the architecture of the lairds and the crofters, he also plundered the cottages of East

Anglia and the south, plagiarised the oversized chimneys and undersized windows of the English architect C. F. A. Voysey, an incorporated into his work early Celtic imagery and the flat, stylised, Japanese motifs which had already attracted the attention of James Whistler and the London aesthetes. Nothing particularly Scottish in that.

Taken together, what this fashionable compilation of international styles adds up to is more a decorative trademark than anything else, at least by comparison with Lorimer's less imaginative but more literal copying of Baronial sources. When Mackintosh's work was first published, for example, a rumour went round London that it had its roots in the Egyptian Room of the British Museum, while others found it Early Greek in flavour. It is perhaps because of the *lack* rather than the *presence* of a regional identity that the Viennese were able to respond to it so readily, as Peter Vergo points out.

'What we often forget now is that Mackintosh was more famous in the early 1900s on the Continent than in Great Britain. What one sees [after his arrival for the 1900 Sezession Exhibition] is the Austrian designers immediately picking up elements of the Mackintosh style, and their work becoming more geometrical, more rectilinear, more severe in a way. And this influence persists for about four or five years until by 1906, at a time when Mackintosh is grinding to a halt himself, looking for new directions, the Viennese style changes quite dramatically so that by the time the Great War breaks out, all this *Art Nouveau* [which attempted an internationalism that had no obvious historical precedents and could bridge continents] had become very unfashionable indeed.'

But Robert Macleod disagrees. 'Many of Mackintosh's Continental emulators were greatly taken with his decorative details and copied them, but copied them into contexts which he would have deplored. I'm sure I would make enemies among some of the scholars by saying that but it seems to me that many of the direct attributions that can be made from Mackintosh to them are applied to buildings which are in fact traditionally and very often pedantically classical in their bones and in their conception, and which have virtually nothing to do with the way Mackintosh's own buildings were germinated.'

Mackintosh's productive years as an architect lasted from 1896, when, as an employee of Honeyman and Keppie, he submitted the winning design in the competition for the new Glasgow School of Art building, until 1909 when, as a partner in the same firm, he completed the extension to the school. In the following few years, the rate at which he was able to attract new commissions to the

office went steadily down – thanks, in part, to his boorish behaviour. He worked increasingly on his own, and stories are told of
how he would be found in the mornings, slumped at his desk,
surrounded by empty whisky bottles and sheets of exquisite
drawings that he had worked on through the night. In 1913, he
finally gave up his partnership and in 1914 left Glasgow for
Walberswick in Suffolk. This was meant to be a stepping-stone to
Vienna where he expected to recapture the appreciation he had
won ten years earlier, but as with his architecture, so his career,
was jeopardised by larger events – in this case the war in Europe.

In 1915, he moved to Chelsea, doing a last commission – the
Dug Out – for Miss Cranston's Willow Tearooms in Sauchiehall
Street, designing book jackets for the publisher Walter Blackie,
for whom he had built Hill House, Helensburgh, in 1903, and
altering and refurnishing two small properties[1] for W. J. Bassett-
Lowke in Northampton. There were other occasional commissions – fabric designs for Foxton's and Sefton's – but for the most
part, Mackintosh was being supported by his three friends. More
and more of his time was spent on painting – it is said that he was
even mistaken for a German spy on one of his painting trips on the
Suffolk coast – and in his last years, in France, he was exclusively a
watercolourist. But Roger Bilcliffe, manager of the galleries of the
Fine Art Society in Glasgow and Edinburgh, has catalogued
Mackintosh's late works, and he believes his reputation as a
painter has been misrepresented.

'Mackintosh has always been thought of after 1915 as a spent
force, as having nothing to contribute to the history of art or
design. And my own belief is that when he left Glasgow he left it
with the intention of starting a new life. He failed to get to Vienna
because of the outbreak of war, but he was very lucky in having a
very intuitive client in Bassett-Lowke from about 1915 to 1920 who
more or less gave him his head. He was a critical client. If he didn't
like something he'd say: 'Why don't you do it this way? I'd like
that.' Mackintosh completely disregarded his instructions and
designed something different on each occasion. In 1919, he
designed the furniture for the guest bedroom at Derngate. That
furniture was a masterpiece of design. It was much simpler than
anything he'd designed twenty years earlier, and really formed the
basis for a new style that not only Mackintosh could have
developed but other people could have developed too. Sadly he
wasn't able to take it any further.'

[1] 78 Derngate, a small terrace house, and Candida Cottage.

Peter Vergo disagrees. 'There's a polarity which runs through Mackintosh's work. At the same time as he's being criticised in Glasgow, he's winning his biggest commissions. As his reputation becomes greater in the early 1900s he does designs which, like many of his Continental counterparts, remain unexecuted. And then there's the last phase where he effectively stops architecture and design altogether and goes over to painting, which I think is an interesting but deeply unsuccessful phase of his work, and which I would refer to as tragic. I see him as an architect and designer – not as a painter.

'It's rather like the paintings of Arnold Schoenberg. One of the discoveries of recent years is that Schoenberg who we remember as a composer also painted pictures. Art historians have pulled these out and said : "My goodness, this is interesting. Look at the point of comparison with Schiele or Kokoschka." But in the end it is a second career of somebody whose real genius lay elsewhere, and I don't think we would remember Mackintosh at all in the way we do if his work had only consisted of these drawings and watercolours.

'At the same time, I would compare him with somebody like Richard Strauss. Richard Strauss said that he was not a composer of the first rank but that he was a very good composer of the second rank, and I think that Mackintosh was a very good architect of the second rank. It's perhaps a little unfair to use the word "superficial", and yet so much of his art is concerned with surface effect that perhaps it's not so unfair after all, since his concern lay with the appearance of a piece of furniture or an interior at the expense of the comfort and utility of the people using it. I think these are very important elements in Mackintosh's work. I would describe him as a limited genius, a genius with a limited appeal, very rooted in his time, and thus lacking the stamina of the truly great artist in whom each succeeding generation finds something new to discover.'

But perhaps this is. The current wave of interest in Mackintosh shows that his appeal is far from limited and that a succeeding generation *has* found something new in him – including Peter Vergo himself – though the reasons for this may have less to do with Mackintosh than with other issues – the perceived rape of Glasgow by its planners after its destruction by German (perhaps even Viennese) bombers in the last war, the motorway madness that destroyed the old tenement districts, and a general, nationwide nostalgia for the old – particularly an old that has been mistreated, like Mackintosh and his buildings.

On the other hand, it was fashion that brought Mackintosh to prominence in his own time and it may only be fashion which has brought him back to prominence in ours. His new popularity seems to be more the result of pressures within society than of a new artistic sensibility. To that extent, he is a mascot for the dispossessed, and when he has served his time, he may again be relegated to the second ranks, as Peter Vergo suggests, along with Richard Strauss and Arnold Schoenberg's paintings.

Nevertheless, for the moment, the Mackintosh phenomenon is in full flood. Like an evangelical crusade, devotees are united by their need to believe in *something*, and to be seen to be believing. Doubts about Mackintosh's eminence are unthinkable. So too is a larger question still to be addressed: not that we only recognise messiahs after they have been crucified – that is just a matter of insensitivity – but that we insist on recognising as messiahs those who *have* been crucified. Charles Rennie Mackintosh is clearly enjoying a second coming but we must not jump to conclusions about why his tomb was empty.

Walter Gropius's Crystal Visions

In the spring of 1979, I failed to meet Tom Wolfe in New York. He had been invited to give the keynote address at the forthcoming annual conference of the Royal Institute of British Architects, held jointly that year with the Society of Industrial Artists and Designers, and I wanted to get hold of a synopsis of what he would be saying. I stood on a noisy street corner in Lower Manhattan, a block or so down from the Woolworth Building, phoning and rephoning in an attempt to break through the stubborn resistance of his answering service. No, Mr Wolfe was not available. No, he was out of town. No, I could not speak to him direct. Yes, they would leave a message. Yes, they would have him call me.

Have a nice day.

I wrote again a couple of months later with the same request, and received a polite reply, written ('penned' or 'scribed' would perhaps be the preferred American usage) in a profusely ornate handwriting that was quite as elaborate and orotund as his prose, but surprisingly un-chic. In fact, it was a rather inartistic script, the decorative swirls and flourishes more cacographic than calligraphic. And brown ink! – not exactly the last word in sophistication. The overall effect was more stilted than elegant. I did not get my synopsis.

The title of the conference at which Mr Wolfe was to speak was *Frontiers of Design*, and the intention of its joint sponsorship was to bring architects and designers together to locate the cutting edge in their respective arts. This, Tom Wolfe did for them within seconds of his arrival, without even opening his mouth. Swanning in in his familiar double-breasted wide-lapelled narrow-twill ice-cream-coloured suit, he represented an unspoken argument for the power of the image as a marketing tool. Not that the competition was all that strong; he was introduced to the audience by their avuncular chairman Lord Reilly, a former Director of the Design Council, who padded about on the rostrum in a baggy grey suit and brown suede shoes. Some things in the exciting, forward-looking world of British design would clearly never change.

The intention of Mr Wolfe's address was the reassertion of bourgeois American values. It was to applaud Islip, Long Island and the San Fernando Valley where, as he said in his lecture, there were pitched roofs and shingles, and mailboxes set up on lengths of stiffened chain that seemed to defy gravity, and wall-to-wall carpet that you could lose a shoe in. This was the real America, the architectural expression of the century in which America had become the richest nation in all history, with a wealth that reached down to every level of the population. This was America's Louis-Bourbon romp.

Tom Wolfe had been writing about the 'real' America for some years – the America of customised cars and customised stars and other wonders of urban life enthusiastically dismissed by the English as the mark of cultural immaturity. But to talk on the printed page about American frivolity was one thing; to talk out loud about architecture was quite another. Architecture was a *serious* subject, a subject supported by social theory and aesthetic typology, and not to be treated lightly, especially before architects and designers who never had treated it lightly.

Before getting round to a revaluation of the American bourgeois tradition, Wolfe had to show how the idea of bourgeoisdom – that is, the American sense of self-worth – had been reviled. He dated the collapse from 1919, when young American architects, artists, and writers transplanted to Europe by the war, found themselves so dazzled by the romantic image of the European intellectual, standing out 'like Gustav Miklos figurines' against the smoking rubble, that they tried to create the same conditions in their own cities. Their efforts were especially helped, Wolfe went on, by the expulsion from Nazi Germany of Walter Gropius, the founder of the Bauhaus, and other Bauhaus luminaries whose arrival in America he compared to that of Bruce Cabot and Myrna Loy crash-landing in the jungle in their safari blouses and jodhpurs, only to be greeted by prostrating savages with bones through their noses chanting that the White Gods had arrived.

The main thrust of the talk was to blame Americans for their servility to what he regarded as the socialist ideology of the Bauhaus: an easy target to take pot shots at in America, but less of a sitting duck in Britain. (We had just had five years of socialist government; the Welfare State was thirty years old. We might even be fellow travellers.) The socialism of the Bauhaus meant, he said, that its highest goal was the creation of perfect worker housing, meaning housing which looked anti-bourgeois and remained resistant to the trappings of upward mobility. Such housing might be fine for pre-war German artisans, but it was out of place in America, especially in a century when 'the energies and idle pleasures of even the working classes became enormous, lurid, creamy, preposterous.' But Wolfe was talking in London, where the energies and idle pleasures of even the working classes had *not* become enormous, lurid, creamy, preposterous; perhaps worker housing *was* appropriate over here. By American standards, we had not, after all, been in the economic running for some time now.

Wolfe's second line of attack was to debunk the White Gods, which he did with wicked humour. Few lectures delivered at the Royal Institute can ever have been so sharp, so irreverent and so delicious. Unfortunately, his came immediately after lunch when even the best minds in the audience were finding it hard not to succumb to the soporific of the food, the wine, and the warm darkness of the Florence Hall, so that not all the references to Myrna Loy and the Long Island aesthetic drew the laughter they deserved. There were even reservations afterwards about whether it had been wise to invite Wolfe to make his exquisitely tailored off-the-cuff remarks in his exquisitely tailored off-the-cuff suit about men whose ideas still permeated the architecture of most of the audience in the hall. Perhaps, once again, he had misjudged the relationship of the British to the White Gods.

It was, nonetheless, a terrific performance, with Mr Wolfe huffing and puffing at the persistence of Americans to treat the worker-housing aesthetic with a respect it did not deserve, and blowing it in with apparently little resistance. 'Many people are beginning to wonder why it is that every American under the age of forty has gone to school in a building that looks like an Addressograph Replacement-Parts Distribution Warehouse,' he told his audience. 'People are beginning to wonder why it is that every new $400,000 home that's built on the shores of Long Island has so many plain, white, pipe railings and so many hob-tread, spiral staircases, and so much industrial plate-glass that they all look like the main engine room of the Grand Teton dam. I know that I personally am beginning to wonder why it is that everybody in my business in New York either lives in, or wants to live in, the same apartment. You see it in every magazine. This apartment always has pure white walls in the living room and, fuel shortage or no fuel shortage, you always find about 4000 watts of R30 spotlights encased in white canisters suspended from what is known as track lighting. There's usually in this apartment a set of Corbusier bentwood chairs which nobody sits in because they catch you like a karate chop in the middle of your back. Nevertheless they're there because they're also in the permanent design collection of the Museum of Modern Art. At dinner time there's brought out a set of Mies' famous stainless-steel S-shaped cane-bottomed dining-room side chairs which are among the three most famous chairs of the twentieth century but also among the most disastrously designed, so that before the end of the dinner at least one guest is always pitched face-forward into the lobster bisque. . . .'

It was a smart talk. And in the following months, it went through a number of transformations, appearing first as a series of articles in American *Harper's* and then in 1982 as a best-selling book, *From Bauhaus to Our House*. With each transformation, Wolfe's brisk one-liners became more extravagant. The 4000 watts of track lighting that he had referred to in London had risen to 17,000 watts by the time the revision came out in its American form. The $400,000 house had gone up to $900,000. Mies' S-shaped chair had become the *second* most famous chair after his Barcelona model, and the total of disastrous designs had risen to five. The exuberant inflation of America's Louis-Bourbon romp obviously applied as much to its literary as to its economic life. This was conspicuous consumption in the raw.

What Mr Wolfe found particularly difficult to come to terms with in the European conspiracy was Walter Gropius. Here was a man who was 'simply but meticulously groomed, correct and urbane, a lieutenant of cavalry during the war, decorated for valour', so aristocratic in his bearing that he was known as 'the Silver Prince'. And here he was, making a profession out of knocking the bourgeoisie. It was a crime! It was a waste! 'Since just about everyone involved was himself bourgeois in the literal, social sense of the word, "bourgeois" became an epithet that meant whatever you wanted it to mean.' In the end, 'Gropius's interest in "the proletariat" or "socialism" turned out to be nothing more than aesthetic or fashionable.'

This was rich, coming from Wolfe, whose equal but opposite interest in the bourgeoisie has been just as much a pose – a detached literary stance, enabling him to string together his neck-laces of adjectives in imitation of that 'full-blooded, go-to-hell, belly-rubbing, wahoo-yahoo, youthful rampage' of middle America without ever personally subscribing to its values. He has flirted with the crass and the vulgar, but as an observer, an outsider, and while his manner in print is loud and ostentatious, it is also knowing, for Wolfe is both a Yankee-doodle dandy and a witty, urbane Southern university intellectual who has made a speciality out of his engagement with Bad Taste.

Wolfe's talk highlighted, nevertheless, the twofold problem of how one approaches Gropius – the man himself, and what came after him – and in this, he performed the useful task of moving the argument on from the general complaint about the appearance of Gropius' buildings to something more specific: that Gropius and his kind were not wanted in the USA, and that they had no place stepping outside Europe – perhaps not even outside Germany. Was he right?

Walter Gropius was born in 1883 of an architectural family in Berlin. In 1908 he joined the office of Peter Behrens where, for a while, he worked alongside Mies van der Rohe and Le Corbusier. The previous year, Behrens had helped to found the Deutscher Werkbund, an association of artists, craftsmen, academics and industrialists concerned with the reform of art and design edu-cation, the propagation of art in an industrial society, and the development of Germany's cultural and economic power. Gro-pius found Behrens and the Werkbund an enormous influence, and many of his later ideas are directly attributable to this experience.

As an independent architect from 1910, his style owed much to the stripped classicism of Behrens, but working with Adolph Meyer he was also capable of designing some of the prototypes of modern architecture. He had already developed plans for mass-produced housing, and in 1913 he published an article in the Deutscher Werkbund *Jahrbuch* praising the simplicity of American grain silos. His model factory at the Werkbund exhibition the next year led Henri van de Velde, then head of the School of Applied Arts in Weimar, to nominate him as his successor. The school, however, was dissolved in 1915 while Gropius was serving in the war and it was not until 1919 that he was appointed to take over both the applied and fine arts schools in Weimar and merge them into a new institution – the Bauhaus.

Under Gropius's leadership, the Bauhaus acquired an international reputation as a forward-thinking, radical force, changing the face of architecture and industrial design. Gropius too became a figurehead for a new style of thinking and a new aesthetic: efficiency, functionalism, mechanisation – these were the watchwords he came to represent. But that is only half the story, and an inaccurate half. In his running of the Bauhaus, as in all else, Gropius was the prodigal son of German Romanticism – 'The German disease' – originally a nineteenth century protest movement against the French Enlightenment, finally the breeding ground of Nazism. The Romantics believed that rationalism and intellectuality were stifling to creativity and the human spirit. They believed that there were aspects of life that defied scientific analysis, and that instinct was a better guide to the deeper truths than reason. Where the French *philosophes* were concerned with modernity and progress, the Germans made a cult out of origins and folklore, venerating the individual Genius and his right to realise his potential even at the expense of the community.

Gropius was part of a national reaction against this hundred-year-old tradition, and it was an important reaction, coming at a time – just after the Great War – when Germany needed urgently to pick itself up, clear out the detritus of the old century, and take up the challenge of the new. Like many of his contemporaries, he stood opposed to the dark, mysterious, emotional appeal of Romanticism, looking with a fresh and appreciative eye at utilitarianism, reason and progress. However, his attitude to the new scientific age was coloured by the Romanticism he came out of, so that he was always to be driven by an emotional vision of what that scientific age might achieve. In the same way, although the new virtues he subscribed to appeared to be rational, they exercised as mystical a power over him as those they superseded. Furthermore, the process of casting out old ideas and heralding in new ones was a slow one, and depended on who Gropius was in contact with and being influenced by, so that there was always some confusion about what he did or did not believe in.

Gropius's grip on the Bauhaus lasted until 1928 when he resigned. During that period, he introduced some of the most revolutionary artists in Europe as teachers, only to find that the interest they aroused became a threat to his own authority. At the same time, he needed those artists to give the school its direction. 'Let us conceive, consider and create together the new buildings of the future,' he wrote in the first Bauhaus manifesto, 'that will bring all into one single integrated creation: architecture, painting and sculpture rising to Heaven out of the hands of a million craftsmen, the crystal symbol of a new faith in the future.' It was inspiring, but it was not necessarily clear what it meant for the day-to-day running of the place.

'The fundamental thing about Gropius,' says the architecture critic Charles Jencks, 'is that he was very conscious, like Oswald Spengler and all those Germans at the end of the First World War, that western culture had broken down, and the Bauhaus was in a sense a new, primitivist, Christian sect that would rise up from the ground and unify all classes of society into a new spiritualism, a new religion, but a religion he could never name because there was no content to it. It was a vague theosophy, a vague spiritualism which he hoped would unify a disintegrated culture. He didn't see, though, that it was a spiritualism without a priestly class and without a theology. He never understood that you have to believe in something – it's not just abstract God or abstract Nature.'

Gropius was not alone, however, in wanting to unite the nation in this way. Throughout Europe, radical groups were springing up and making similarly messianic promises for art or society or both – the Futurists in Italy with their worship of war and the machine; the Expressionists in Germany with their talk of ethereal cities of glass and light; the more painterly Purists in France, turning ordinary objects into abstract 'types'; and the de Stijl group in Holland, whose interests lay with lines and rectangles. Gropius, never an originator, acted as a magnifying mirror to those things that were nearest at hand, picking up their styles of oratory and their preoccupations and incorporating them.

In its first years, the Bauhaus operated like an Expressionist vision of a medieval guild, with teachers known as Masters. Gropius saw the school as a radiant cathedral – an image represented in a woodcut by Lyonel Feininger, one of the staff, on the cover of the first manifesto. Inside the cathedral, all students, whether artists or craftsmen, would undergo the same preliminary training – the *Vorkurs* – directed by the Swiss painter and mystic,

Johannes Itten. This was rather like going back to kindergarten. Conventional teaching had to be unlearnt. The course focused on developing the personality, liberating innate abilities, and cultivating the intuition. There was also a lot of garlic chewing, for inner health (the wife of Laszlo Moholy-Nagy, who came to the Bauhaus in 1923, recalled in later years that this was the most characteristic feature of the school and its students). In the same breath, students were introduced to ideas about universality and spiritual harmony, and to the teachings of Mazdaznan, Tao and Zen. As Gropius was to say in later years: 'Develop an infallible technique; then put yourself at the mercy of heavenly inspiration.'

The problem for the young *Bauhäusler* was to discover the source of divine guidance when there was no acknowledgement of a Divinity. For the original *Bauhütte* – the medieval communities of cathedral builders after whom the Bauhaus was named – the very act of building was a gesture of group dedication to God. But communal participation at Weimar depended on Gropius's presence as cult-leader to give it meaning. The meaning he gave it, being an architect, was to deify the process of architecture, which he described as 'a sovereign federative union' in which all the subordinate arts took their appointed place, like planets, sun and stars circling the earth in a Ptolemaic heaven. God as Architect had become the architect as God, bringing order to artistic chaos. To be confirmed as that divine architect, one went to Gropius.

It was a noble duty that Gropius performed, and one to which he brought all the virtues that Tom Wolfe stressed and all the inconsistencies that Charles Jencks worries about. 'Deep down,' says Jencks, 'Gropius was a mystical character who liked to sing Christmas carols to the young students, dress up as Santa Claus, take them out in the woods, and put on performances. He was that kind of romantic father-figure who was later suppressed by the other side of his character. He had two sides to him, and the Rationalist side got the better of the Expressionist side, but underneath it all, he was the Pied Piper, he was the fiddler who liked to play, but he was too grave a person ever to allow himself to play. His nickname in the famous Expressionist days was *Maas*, meaning "measure", and when you look at portraits of him, he always looks very stern and measured. Of all those Expressionists, he was the severe father-figure – the one who wouldn't let himself go.'

Gropius did not let go because he was having to hold on so tight. Itten's mystical ideas were more attractive to the students than Gropius's dry interest in technology, and this created internal tensions. Then, in 1922, a visiting lecturer – Theo van Doesburg of the de Stijl group – swung the students towards more Cubist, geometrical pursuits. It was only with Moholy-Nagy's arrival the following year that Gropius was able to direct the teaching more toward industrial design, publishing a memorandum in 1924 called *Art and Technology – A New Unity*. This of course was a *new* new unity.

Gropius's architecture reflected these changes in the same way. He had reverted in the years just after the war from the industrial imagery of his Werkbund pavilion to a far more Expressionist style. With the changes at the Bauhaus in 1923, he was to change again, this time working in a new synthesis between his factory aesthetic of 1914 and the Cubism of van Doesburg. The new style was put into effect in 1926; Weimar had always regarded the Bauhaus as a community of undesirables and in 1925 the school was dissolved. The following year Gropius designed new purpose-built accommodation in Dessau.

The Dessau building was a collection of large, white boxes with flat roofs and vast walls of glass framed in long, white surrounds. On appearance alone, it seemed the ultimate in advanced construction, but this was a contrivance, for its walls were made in the most traditional way, using stucco on brickwork. It is perhaps more useful to think of it as a hand-crafted prototype for a technology which did not yet exist, and one which invited the observer by its unconventional appearance to speculate on what the nature of that technology might be. This is how it is read by Norman Foster, the 1983 Royal Gold Medallist for Architecture. 'At the level of bringing architecture back to its craft roots, of having honourable roots in the production process, it was radical because you were getting production processes that had the potential to alienate, and what Gropius and Adolph Meyer were really saying was that they can be benign.'

Dessau made unconventional use of available technology to evoke a new era. In that sense, it was a piece of late Expressionist symbolism, for its conception was a work of *visual* rather than *technical* imagination. It was symbolic also in its disposition. The workshop and library blocks were separated by a road but linked by an administrative bridge – a bridge which mediated spiritually, like Maria in Fritz Lang's film of the same year, *Metropolis*, between the working masses and the thinking elite. It was a representation of the new society in which hand and brain were joined by the heart. But it was also a representation of Gropius's position – committed to the welfare of all sides but caught between them.

In 1927, Hannes Meyer arrived at the Bauhaus as head of a new department of architecture, a subject which had never actually been properly taught before in spite of Gropius's presence. Meyer immediately took over the role of Pied Piper, spiriting the students out of Gropius's control, and turning the school into a Marxist nursery. The following year Gropius resigned, together with Moholy-Nagy, the typographer Herbert Bayer, and Marcel Breuer who had run the furniture course. All three were to assist him on designs for the Deutscher Werkbund exhibition in Paris two years later.

Back in Berlin, Gropius designed furniture and became in 1929 the vice-president of CIAM (the Congrès Internationaux d'Architecture moderne), but found himself under increased pressure when the Nazis came to power in 1933. He responded characteristically with a bid for appeasement, writing to Goebbels personally to say that he had been misrepresented, that he came from a family of architects steeped in the work of Schinkel, that his architecture was loyal to the Fatherland, and that it was not the same as the Marxists were doing. As ever, Gropius tried to fit in.

Italian architects were under similar pressures. An approximation of the Bauhaus style had been made into the official architecture of the Fascist party until Mussolini capitulated to German pressure; then, along with the adoption of the Nuremberg race laws, the new, progressive style was rejected in favour of the monumental classicism of Albert Speer. Gropius's appeal on behalf of culture was equally ineffective and even as Goering reached for his revolver, Gropius was snatched away to safety by Jack Pritchard, an English entrepreneur and patron of modern design, and the architect Maxwell Fry, who offered him a partnership in his office. Gropius arrived in England in 1934, at the age of fifty-one, but quickly moved on to America. All the signs were that the creative part of his career was now over. He had lost the Bauhaus, but more important, he had lost the initiative.

'His work was done when he came to me,' reflects Maxwell Fry. 'Substantially done. He did a little designing with me at the Village College [in Impington, Cambridgeshire]. He goes on to America where he's completely submerged into the system. His impact there is minimal. I mean, America is massively commercial. I was astonished, talking to Gropius in later years at Harvard, that his firm could actually go out and seek work and bid for it. I couldn't have imagined doing such a thing. I am by comparison a highly professional person who stands ready to be used but would think it beneath my dignity to go and get [work] – even to go to a golf club.

But it was a different world he got into and I don't think he had any conception of it when he went.'

The American architect Ioh Ming Pei agrees – and disagrees. 'I think he was absolutely exhilarated by the New World. It was like a breath of fresh air. There seemed to be so much to do. People – not just architects – were very receptive to some of the ideas that he had, witness the fact that he was able to attract students from all over the world, not just the United States. His ideas and the ideas of those who came with him actually took hold rather quickly and I think he was surprised by that. He expected more opposition.'

Gropius had put up with English professionalism for three long years before heading west to take up a professorship at the Harvard Graduate School of Design. From having been written off as a back number, he was once again, at the age of fifty-four, a man of action. 'We were without much direction at that time,' I. M. Pei recalls. 'The Beaux-Arts system at the school was somewhat in disrepute and our professors were no longer giving us the kind of leadership we expected, and Gropius provided that very strong sense of direction.'

'Harvard had followed fairly closely the Beaux-Arts education of Paris,' agrees Gropius's biographer Reg Isaacs who was already a student at Harvard when Gropius took up his new post. 'It was very much like the education in fifteen or twenty other US schools, each boasting a French diplômé – a "genuine Frenchman" and graduate of the Beaux-Arts School. It was taken for granted that one would follow the classic orders. We knew that if we wanted to complete the course, our work would have to be classical and that innovation would have to come within the bounds of classic design. When Gropius came to Harvard of course it was fertile ground. In fact it was probably circumstantial that it was Gropius rather than Le Corbusier, for example, who was sought and brought to the States. They were looking for a new leader and there was a depression and we couldn't afford to build in the classic manner that we had for decades before.'

The reasons which made Gropius right for Harvard were very similar to those which had made him right for Weimar in 1919: the need for leadership, the climate of depression, the unhealthy economy. And, as in Weimar, he was regarded with some scepticism – at least, initially. 'I think the existing establishment found him threatening,' says I. M. Pei. 'Many schools were in disarray and of course Gropius made them uncomfortable. That competition was very good for them; it actually caused many of them to change their curricula. But what Gropius was not able to challenge were our financial institutions and in those years it was extremely difficult to get a mortgage for a house with a flat roof. I tried it – it was impossible. It took much longer for Gropius's idea to prevail in that larger scheme of things.

'But I don't believe there were any fears for the political implications of the architecture he was bringing over. There was a certain leftist tendency among many of those [European] practitioners but I tend to look at them as apolitical. Certain planning principles put heavy emphasis on social concerns, particularly in the field of planning, but that's not bad. In fact I don't think our planners were in disagreement; I think some of our pioneer planners were already espousing ideas of that kind before Gropius came. When you talk about planning, you can't help but think in terms somewhat to the left.'

The paradox of Gropius's situation is that his radical ideas were able to be absorbed so rapidly. The more socialist of his contemporaries who had fled from Nazi Germany to the Soviet Union were suppressed under Stalin and never heard of again. In the America of Roosevelt – even, later, in the America of McCarthy – their counterparts from the Bauhaus were to thrive. No doubt if Tom Wolfe had known then what he knows now, he would have been reporting Gropius to the House Committee on Un-American Activities. But there would have been no need. Gropius's reaction to Hannes Meyer at Dessau had shown where his political affiliations did *not* lie, and his sympathies did not greatly change when he found himself at Harvard.

Wilhelm von Moltke, whose father was hanged for his part in the failed 'Officers' Plot' to assassinate Hitler, was a student of Gropius in America. 'I'm quite sure that the FBI looked with displeasure at what he did,' he says. 'We published a magazine called *TASK*, and one issue I remember was on housing in Russia, and we were very proud of it and quite defiant about traditional American values. But Gropius didn't always like what we did because we criticised one of his houses – the Frank House in Pittsburgh which he did together with Marcel Breuer.[1] It was a rather vulgar, pretentious, rich man's house and you could just smell the wealth in it. We criticised it for not being "social" enough and he wasn't happy about that!'

As far as Gropius being a threat was concerned, the soil of

[1]Breuer joined Gropius in America, working in partnership with him from 1938 to 1941.

America had converted the potentially revolutionary into the merely novel. As late as the 1960s, he could still write in his most manifestly manifesto style that it was time for the individual – but not 'the artist' or 'the masses', note – to take to the barricades and fight the forces of chaos and confusion that emanated from cheap commercialism and sophisticated salesmanship. But it was no more threatening than any New England revivalist preacher holloaing from his pulpit; it was exactly how America expects to be spoken to by its moral leaders.

England, by contrast, acted the perfect host but never warmed to its guest, whose manners were equally impeccable. Had he stayed here, he might at most have joined the ranks of the Great and the Good, sat in on the birth of the Welfare State, and given his blessing to the New Town boom. 'He liked this country very much,' says Maxwell Fry. 'It was a revelation to him. I mean, he thought when he met intelligent members of the Conservative Party that they were raging socialists, and so they were compared to Germany! But if he'd stayed on, and he knew the war would happen, we would have put him in the Isle of Man. I knew that. And Harvard became more and more insistent and first of all they sent over Joseph Hudnut and then finally Conant, the president, came in person to say "Gropius, we will give you everything if you come to Harvard." And of course, he had to accept.'

In America, there were opportunities to practise and preach; in England, only to preach. 'On his first visit to London in 1930, he had delivered a speech which had been translated by Morton Shand in what Morton called his *dense* German, and it was very humourless, very voluminous, but it was nevertheless electric and extremely moving, not only on account of the address itself but of the man giving it. He told us of the responsibility we had to create art out of a world that was dominated by industry and science – that out of this we could get fit materials for an art; in fact, that we could give industry its marching instructions. It was a very great message' – especially if you happened to be an architect.

But its greatness relied on its being implemented, and that was more difficult to achieve. Jack Pritchard tried to concoct schemes to keep Gropius busy but the only one that paid off was the Village College at Impington. This was taken up after the war as a model for school-building on account of its large 'health-giving' windows and two-source lighting, its leaf-and-branch pattern of rooms and corridors, and its single-storey layout.

Impington redefined the way in which a school was organised and used. It identified places where necessary duplication could be introduced. It also made various assumptions about how English village life would develop, predicting that in the future, everyone would have a car. This meant that Impington could become the focus of communal resources for several outlying villages, with considerable economies of scale being achieved. In addition, it provided for the educational and cultural activities of adults as well as children by treating the building as a community centre instead of simply as a school.

Exactly how much of this thinking came from Gropius rather than Maxwell Fry is impossible to tell. What can be observed, though, is that it was much more an English empirical scheme than a German ideological transplant. It was very sure of what it valued – health, education, communal activity, sunlight, economic and moral good sense – but it relied for its success less on a sense of shared vision than on chummy goodwill. When Henry Morris, Cambridgeshire's then Director of Education, found that he could not justify paying for Gropius's fees because the county had its own Architect's Department, he immediately asked Jack Pritchard to send him the draft of a begging letter in his own name, which he could sign, calling on sympathetic friends to sponsor Gropius privately. Impington might have been an assault on the old-fashioned Greyfriars kind of institution, but there was nevertheless something rather wizard-wheezey about the 'Let's Find Work for Gropius' campaign.

In Jack Pritchard's yarns about the 'Illustrious Emigré,' Gropius figures as the German answer to Huree Jamset Ram Singh, the Nabob of Bhanipur. 'On one occasion,' Pritchard remembers, 'we were motoring down to Devon and we drove past huge posters by the road which said: "You are entering the Strong country" and "Take Courage". And Gropius, who had only recently left a Germany that was awash with political slogans, began to get more and more agitated, and started saying "What's happening to this country?" It was only when we stopped at a pub and he saw the label on the beer that he realised his mistake!'

Impington was one attempt at a reappraisal of a traditional form which paid off. Others did not, but the three pals still continued to explore architectural forms that were so much a caricature of English life that they, too, could have come out of the *Magnet*. Among the ventures which never came to anything was one for Windsor Great Park. 'Our idea,' Jack Pritchard says, 'was to simulate what happened in the great days of the country houses where there'd be the family and relatives and all their servants. We thought, let us build a mansion but make it a modern building with a very high standard of features and of course the people, the workers, would live on the estate. Molly, my wife, wrote a very careful brief of the kind of people that were going to live in the building.'

What was stipulated? 'The obvious things – people who were well off.'

So this wasn't one of Tom Wolfe's worker-housing schemes? 'Oh Lord, no! Windsor wasn't workers' housing. It was for people, we speculated, with about £500 a year, which in those days was a lot of money.'

The Gropius of England was clearly not the same man as the Gropius of Germany had been, or the Gropius of America was going to be, so overshadowed was he – as always – by the company he kept. The only threat he constituted lay in his reputation – which persisted. 'It was very interesting,' says Jack Pritchard. 'We had a great farewell dinner party before he left for America, and I couldn't help feeling an undercurrent of "Yes, Gropius is a very great man; thank goodness he's not going to disturb our status quo anymore."'

It was in America that Gropius finally proved himself the chameleon. Having no real identity of his own, he could be an extremely effective teacher – encouraging his students without giving them specific direction. Chip Harkness studied under Gropius at Harvard and worked as his teaching assistant before setting up with him in a collaborative architects' practice. 'What is great about Grope,' says Harkness, 'is not that he taught a particular *style* but that he tried to teach an *approach* which would have infinite potential. I think what he was teaching really included the points of view of Le Corbusier and Mies. Probably the best and most used books at that time were Corbu's [*Complete Works*]. Those were very much on everyone's desk for reference because those had formalistic ideas. So when you were looking for an answer to your problem you tended to look to a book like that. You couldn't look to Grope other than, say, to the Bauhaus and a few things like that. You couldn't crib forms from him. He wasn't selling forms.'

The absence of original forms in Gropius's work was just as much a problem for Gropius as it was for his students; he also needed designs to crib from. Having absorbed the architecture of Behrens, Meyer, van Doesburg and the Expressionists in Germany, and attempted to reinterpret the pattern of country life with Maxwell Fry in England, his architecture in America was again to rely on the styles of the people he was working with. Together with Marcel Breuer, his domestic buildings in New England reflect elements of local character, combining the advantages of modern construction (catalogue metal windows, flat roof terraces, and pillars for raising parts of the house and freeing the space below) with the overall proportions, the light wooden-frame construction, and the traditional materials (wooden shingles and external random stone chimneys) of the New England farmhouse tradition. His own house at Lincoln, Mass., is built in this way – obviously modern, but different enough from the white Cubist architecture of Germany for Lewis Mumford to describe it as the most regional building he had ever seen.

Gropius's larger buildings in America and elsewhere were carried out in partnership with a group of former students including Chip Harkness, his wife Sally, and Norman Fletcher. After graduating in 1945, they had invited Gropius to join them on equal pay and equal terms in an experimental firm called 'The Architects' Collaborative', or 'TAC' – an offer which he readily accepted. Norman Fletcher believes that Gropius was well aware of playing a catalytic rather than a leaderhip role. 'He liked to think of himself as a catfish in a boat. The analogy being that the fisherman comes back from a haul at sea over many hours, and tries to keep the fish fresh. So he always keeps a catfish in the boat to keep them all jumping and alive until they get back to harbour. He fancied himself as the catfish in the boat.'

It is almost embarrassing to have to admit that among the buildings that the catfish inspired were the Pan-Am Building in New York and the Playboy Club in London. To some extent, Gropius' responsibility for these is mitigated by their being group projects. But if there is shared responsibility, there is also shared blame, and the loyal I. M. Pei finds it difficult even to enter into discussion of these later works. 'I would say that his architecture in America is best represented by his residences, and of those his own is the best of the lot because it's so much *him*. It's probably one of the best examples of experimenting with latching new ideas onto an existing vernacular. At the same time, its spatial manipulation and detailing are first class. If you refer to later, urban buildings, you are talking about TAC; you're not talking about Gropius anymore. And TAC's architecture is not the subject of this conversation.'

Pei's natural diplomacy and his respect for his former teacher do not disguise the fact that in dissociating Gropius from the work of TAC, he is denying one of the central planks of Gropius's teaching – the idea of collaboration. Collaborative working as an expression of social unity was drilled into the students at the Bauhaus and Harvard, and with time it has become a standard practice in many areas of American industry. But to Pei, the tug of American individualism remains stronger; even in the modern world, beyond the reach of German Romanticism, it is comforting to know that there are heroes.

The corollary of the hero is the villain, and where heroes are a comfort to have around, villains are a consolation to point the finger at. Charles Jencks blames Gropius not just for collaborating with TAC but for being a collaborator in a world-wide conspiracy to promote the most destructive architectural style ever seen. 'Everyone did it, and did it so badly and polluted the environment with second-rate buildings. We've never had more second-rate buildings in the history of the world than after the International Style.'

At the same time, Jencks acknowledges that the success of Modernism in terms of its prevalence had very little to do with Gropius at all. 'The reasons modern architecture lasted so long are really negative: that it became the easiest style for the bureaucracies to use, it became the easiest style to copy, the cheapest style, and it was simply the most moronic style around. That's why it lasted: because morons could produce it for morons, turning people into morons by using it. I'm exaggerating, but in a way, the success of Modernism is dubious at best; its success in a sense is its failure' – or, equally, its failure is its success.

That does not, however, let Gropius off the hook. 'He's partly responsible for the degradation of our Modernist environment, that watered-down International Style,' says Dr Jencks. 'He proselytised for it, he helped it go round the world, and he didn't see how it denied his fundamental message of creativity, of individuality of the spirit. He always used to state, for instance, when I knew him, that some day those anonymous houses which were so impersonal would have what he called their *moss of humanity* which would grow over them organically and humanise them. Well, I think that that was sad wishful thinking. He must have known in his heart that the new-town blues and those impersonally mass-produced monoliths were never going to be humanised. Whether he knew that at the beginning, I don't know. I guess he didn't; if he had done he would, I think, have reacted differently. [The problem was that] the great proselytisers of Modernism had an ideology of never failing, and in the world of architecture when millions of dollars or pounds are involved, you can't have failures otherwise you'll get sued by our client. And one has to feel sorry for architects; they have to claim they're always right. It's a disaster.'

Architecture means never having to say you're sorry – and Gropius never did. In private, he may have expressed doubts about his work, but there never was a public confession nor was he burned at the stake of any anti-Modernist inquisition. So the anger against mid-twentieth-century architecture still attaches to him as a scapegoat. Perhaps if he had donned sackcloth, scattered ashes over his head, scourged himself in the centre of Harvard Yard, and walked backwards on his hands and knees to Weimar, he might have done something to appease the loathing he inspires. Even an acknowledgement that all was not well with the state of architecture might have gone some way to silence the critics. But he did not.

The charges against Gropius are that he was self-deluding, misguided and complacent, and that he produced an architecture so debased that it devastated the world. But Gropius never taught architecture as such; as Chip Harkness has said, and as I. M. Pei remembers, he never taught forms, only principles. And the principles were good ones. 'He was against any sham,' says Pei, 'and that was important. Back in the early 1940s, architecture had not yet acquired the luxury of being looked at as an art form, although in Gropius's mind I'm sure it was already very much that. And we started to look at our student designs and asked: "Are they honest? Do they have integrity?" That is what he taught me. Now, after you have found the truth, then you begin to say: "Look here, the truth is more than just honesty." And that came later. And I think those who are questioning him today, and asking whether his teaching was valid, are really speaking with hindsight. They're saying: "Now we have won this battle, can we make it more exciting?" But at that time [it was a case of] looking at our designs, asking whether they had truth, and hoping that from that truth, beauty would come.'

The conventional reconciliation between I. M. Pei's praise for what Gropius taught his students and Charles Jencks' condemnation of what they actually learnt is provided by Chip Harkness. 'There's a difference between whether the ideals were right or wrong and whether the solutions that came out of those ideals were right or wrong,' he says. 'My own opinion is that many of the *solutions* were wrong – that maybe they didn't take enough factors into account. I think it's a fact of nature that it takes a while for things to evolve into a pattern that really makes sense. The Italian village didn't grow up overnight, it took a while to grow. So I think modern architecture simply hasn't had its time yet. It will come.'

If Harkness's speech recalls Gropius's complacency, it may be simply that familiarity breeds contempt. 'When we started off,' he says, 'modern architecture was very unsaleable. As time went by, almost the reverse took effect – namely, that the things Grope stood for and the things he had said were repeated so much that they didn't sound unusual anymore. By the time Grope had made his point and everyone had accepted it, the reaction was: "So what? Everybody knows that." Well, everybody knew that because they had learned it from Grope.'

As a practising architect, however, Gropius was a follower, not a leader. 'Gropius was responsible for putting forward the rational, dry, functionalist stuff,' Charles Jencks admits, 'but one must remember that it was very aristocratic at that point. It was incredibly beautiful. It wasn't as we know it today – dull, depressing, and watered-down. It wasn't so utilitarian. It really had a sharp edge. When you first look at the White Style, you say: "My God, it's more expressive than Expressionism. It's more exciting. It's more dynamic as an art form." And that is what is so fascinating – that one of the reasons Gropius adopts it at that point, as indeed did [Mies, Breuer, Meyer, Oud, Stam *et al*], is that it becomes, as post-Modern classicism is today,[1] the most compelling form-language to work in at the moment, and all the best architects immediately gravitate towards it, give up what they were doing yesterday, and leap on this new express train of history.'

As the years went by, Gropius's work showed no signs of gaining in confidence or independence. 'Great architects from Palladio to Le Corbusier had theories of architecture that didn't allow them to prostitute their art,' says Charles Jencks. 'So that at a certain level, they retained their integrity because this theory could be independent of whatever regime came in. And therefore, although they might be opportunistic on one level (like Le Corbusier, who collaborated with Vichy France), they never compromised their art. Whereas Gropius, as you can see in his late work, would really make a pastiche of other people's work so that his work, at the end, was just a second-rate version of the very thing he was criticising – which was prima-donna, fashionable architecture.

'He produced the great leaders of the next generation of American architecture – Philip Johnson, Olaf Franzen, I. M. Pei, Paul Rudolph, and subsequent people like that. And all of those people more or less rejected his teachings, all became prima donnas, all practised formalism, and all became late-

[1]Charles Jencks was speaking in 1983.

Modernist failures because they didn't produce anything greater than sculpture. And Gropius himself ends up this way. So you have the supreme paradox of a man who is attacking prima donnas and attacking formalism ending up producing both of those things. And I think it was a lack of theory that did it to him. He was a pragmatist.'

But how fair is it to judge him on the basis of the work of his followers? 'His work is worse. The late work of Gropius doesn't have the exuberance of Paul Rudolph or the tenacity of I. M. Pei or the formalism of Philip Johnson, who are convinced formalists. Poor Walter was a sad formalist. He knew he shouldn't be doing what he was doing but he didn't know what else to do. . . .'

What started out as blame ends as regret. It was not that Gropius corrupted his students, or the youth of America, or Tom Wolfe's friends; it was that they corrupted him. He had remained faithful to the principles of Itten's *Vorkurs* at the Bauhaus. He had encouraged his students to develop their personalities, enabled them to bring out their innate skills, and given them the freedom to pursue their own initiatives. He had allowed, in other words, the various worlds he inhabited to express themselves in their own way without telling them how to do it. And they responded in their different ways, thanking him for his trouble and passing him by. If we criticise him now, we are criticising our own expression of ourselves that he enabled us to see.

For his own part, Gropius retained the mysterious ability to see in the ugliness of the modern environment a still-shining crystal symbol of his faith in the future. It may have jeopardised his reason and his art, but that was the German disease.

Sound Unsound

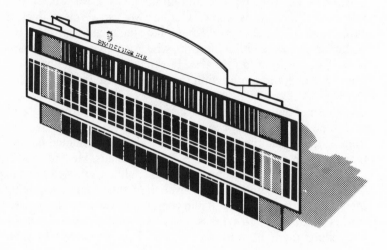

As a student, I used to go to concerts in London at least every week and often twice a week. These days, six months may go by between visits. I suppose this ranks me with former football fans who no longer support their home teams or filmgoers whose lack of attendance has helped to close Essoldos and Gaumonts all round the country. But I find, like them, that what used to be a social event is now perfectly acceptable as a private affair to be enjoyed in the home, and that while there has been an obvious loss of scale and occasion, there are advantages which more than compensate. Radio, records and cassettes do not require undivided attention. I do not have to spend half an hour driving into town only to find all the parking spaces are taken, or wait for the last train on a rain-lashed platform. Nor is there the additional expense (which seems to go with every concert) of a meal for two beforehand and drinks in the interval. There were good reasons why primitive man domesticated the horse and the dog; there are equally good reasons why advanced man has done the same to music, and convenience is one of them. Small wonder, then, that concert-hall attendances are falling off.

Yet concert halls are still being built. In 1983, two major new auditoria opened in Britain – St David's Hall in Cardiff and the Royal Concert Hall in Nottingham. And unlike the film industry, where the big screen has been halved and quartered, these new halls are as large, or larger, than ever. Cardiff contains 2000 seats, Nottingham 2500.

Why are such halls built? Perhaps less as a public service than for reasons of civic pride. The two may be related. On the other hand, the concert hall may also no longer be the best way to flatter mayoral egos. There was a time when a hall could cater solely for the public's demand for music. Today, that public demand has become an individual demand which can be satisfied privately, and more democratically, without the local authority putting an extra burden on the rates to pay for a type of building which may have become an anachronism.

At the Hexagon in Reading, another recently-built hall, the management estimates that the most faithful of its musical devotees will turn up no more than once a week. But the hall must open nightly, and so for the other six nights, orchestral concerts give way to pop, dance (thunderously noisy on a hollow stage), conferences, trade shows and sport – not necessarily because the management wanted to put on a mixed bag of entertainment when the hall was first planned, but because the hall must pay its way.

Concert halls strain for ways to avoid being a public liability in circumstances where live music no longer has the exclusive attraction it once had. Nor do concerts of orchestral music offer the commercial attractions they did in pre-electric days when Patti could ask for, and get, up to £1000 for a single performance.[1] Stars still command inflated sums but concerts now have such limited appeal that they may have to double secretly as rehearsals or promotional exercises for forthcoming recordings, with the costs being paid and if necessary written off by the recording company, if they are to break even.

Changes in economics and fashion have even more far-reaching effects. The nineteenth-century concert hall could seat 1800 people at most. This was a comfortable compromise: intimate enough for Mozart but large enough for Wagner. In addition, such a hall did not make unreasonable demands on the

[1]Patti received £1000 a night on her American tour of 1880, considerably more than the $3000 a night which Dame Nellie Melba was given for appearing in New York in 1906.

physical properties of sound. But a strange inversion of logic takes place in modern concert halls; because of declining audiences, they are built with capacities of 2000 and, if possible, 3000 seats in the hope that the profits from an occasional sell-out will compensate for less popular evenings. The result is that some auditoria are so outlandishly large that chamber music is impossible to perform, while even Berlioz would find himself hard pressed to score a noise sufficiently powerful to fill the space. These architectural juggernauts end up being suited only to those events – conferences and rock concerts – which rely on a public-address system or their own stack of 500-watt speakers – both of which contradict the original demand for a hall which has been tailor-made to enhance the *natural* acoustic.

The very phenomenon of the modern concert hall is therefore somewhat misconceived, so that to complain about the quality of sound in such halls is in a sense to miss the point. And yet there seem to be very many auditoria in which the acoustics are simply inadequate. The ironic thing is that at exactly the same time as the auditorium was becoming a redundant form, so the profession of acoustic consultant came into being. Such consultants ought to have argued against the exploitative requirements being made on the design of new concert halls, and probably there would have been many more acoustically sub-standard halls had the profession not existed; it is difficult to speculate. As it is, however, there are a lot of very unsatisfactory halls – too many, in fact – as acousticians themselves admit. Rupert Taylor is an acoustical consultant and author of a popular primer on the subject[1] – a book which clearly needs to gain an even larger readership than it already has.

'We have an awful lot of bad buildings,' he says. 'For example, there's the dreadful story of the Avery Fisher Hall in New York which was trumpeted to be the be-all and end-all of acoustical design, and had to be stripped back to its brickwork. There have been some ghastly failures. Nothing outstanding has been built since the war. I don't think we've advanced on the achievements of the Renaissance and post-Renaissance architects. I don't think we've really come any further than they have.'

The Avery Fisher Hall began life in 1963 as the Philharmonic Hall – a name which still makes strong acousticians shudder. The previous year, in 1962, its acoustic consultant, Dr Leo Beranek, had written the definitive book on concert-hall acoustics, *Music,*

[1]*Noise*, first published in 1970 by Penguin Books.

Acoustics and Architecture.[1] It offered a theory of design, and supplied comparative data on the world's top sixty concert halls which an indignant Dr Beranek had been inspired to collect after reading an attack on the competence of his profession in the *New Yorker*. The book, which immediately became a classic, included a foreword from the conductor Eugene Ormandy who wrote: 'The climax of the volume is the description of the care taken in the planning of Dr Beranek's own Philharmonic Hall at the Lincoln Center in New York, in which Lady Luck has finally been supplanted by careful analysis and the painstaking application of new but firmly grounded acoustic principles.'

Had Mr Ormandy been a more cautious man, he might have hesitated before flinging down so brazen a gauntlet, especially since the Phil had not yet opened. As it was, Lady Luck picked up the challenge, and marked the hall out as a new monument in the history of musical disasters. The quality of sound was so poor that the building had to be entirely remodelled by a series of architectural witch-doctors, during the course of which it changed its name, possibly as a gesture to sympathetic magic. In cases like this, anything is worth a try.

The Philharmonic was not the only disappointment to hit modern concert-hall design. There was the Royal Festival Hall, for example – the showpiece of the 1951 Festival of Britain exhibition on London's South Bank. In common with many halls of the pre- and post-war years, it was designed to produce a strong 'frontal' acoustic – the sound being directed, in other words, straight at the audience from the stage and ceiling instead of being reflected off the side walls. It was also designed to minimise echo and reduce low-frequency reverberation. Unfortunately, it did all of these things too well. The long, low ceiling bounced the sound into the audience so effectively that it was immediately absorbed, instead of having a chance to develop. This produced a dry acoustic which had to be enriched by a secret system of loudspeakers that were gradually installed six years after it opened.

London has had other concert-hall upsets. Thirty years after the Festival Hall, the newly-opened Barbican Hall had to undergo a complete reassessment and partial refit because of the loss of reverberation in the low-frequency range. Its eccentric collection of ceiling-mounted goldfish bowls, installed specifically for acoustic reasons, was dismantled and experiments were carried out to see whether different seating might improve things. Rupert

[1] Published 1963 in America by Wiley.

Taylor, though not involved, privately suspects that the fault lies not with the seats but with the air-conditioning vents which were positioned beneath them. At another hall which he *has* been working on, he has found that the bass sounds get lost inside the ductwork.

Mistakes such as these seem elementary – and yet they are the fruits of professional expertise. The Barbican, for example, was no impulse decision. A scale model was built and tested in a sound laboratory in Cambridge. No such procedures were available in the nineteenth century when acoustic science was still a gleam in the ear of Hermann von Helmholtz, the pioneer of acoustical and optical research. And yet Victorian concert halls are regarded as more successful. So it appears that as acoustics has become a more sophisticated science, the design of concert halls has got worse. Something must be going seriously wrong. But what?

'When somebody designs a building, they first appoint an architect,' says Rupert Taylor. 'And then they realise they've got to appoint a structural engineer. And then a mechanical services consultant. Then suddenly it dawns on them that they need an acoustical consultant, and he comes in sometimes months after the design has been worked out. And his powers to do what is sometimes necessary – drastic things like changing the shape of the auditorium – are just not available to him. They've probably done so many drawings that nobody's prepared to change them. So he, poor chap, has to play around with the surface materials. When the architect is an acoustician, or when the architect is noble enough to bring in an acoustical consultant right from the start, then great things can be done.'

William Allen, a consultant on the Festival Hall, recognises the problems. 'Leo Beranek did have a misfortune on the Philharmonic Hall and only had five meetings, as I understand it, with the architect during the course of the design. And I believe there was a gap of a year when he didn't have *any* contact with him. When we were working on the Festival Hall, we had two meetings a week. We joined the team on the fourth day and it was total rapport. We had a group of conductors to advise us, and we said: "We think we can give you either clarity or tone. Given the choice, which would you go for?" And they said: "Tone." Well, they got rather a lot of clarity.'

As an advertisement for the great things that can be achieved when acousticians are brought in from the start, William Allen's words somehow lack persuasion, which is sad for the acoustics profession. There they stand, pleading for their expertise, and clutching at small achievements to fend off gargantuan failures, many of which were outside their control to begin with.

Words like 'clarity' and 'tone' point to another failing of acoustics – the absence of an objective terminology. At present, the language of sound is no more reliable – in fact less so – than that of wine tasting. 'It seems to be a rather dry, frontal acoustic without much intimacy or body, but I think you'll be amused by its presence,' an acoustician or a musician might very well say, and he'll expect to be understood. Even expert quaffers like Andrew Porter, former music critic of the *Financial Times*, now of the *New Yorker*, finds that without blind tasting, the ear can be misled.

'When the Philharmonic Hall in New York opened, there was a period when its basic colour was navy blue, which I think simply had a visual effect on the acoustics. It appeared to soak up the sound. And once they had painted it a lighter colour, at the cost of a paint job, they got a very much better *apparent* sound. Carnegie Hall, in the same way, has a feel which makes you feel disposed to enjoy the concert even before the music has begun.

'Alice Tully Hall, on the other hand, is very bleak. It's made of wood and it has almost no architectural features except when the organ stands revealed, and then it gives a focal point at the end of the hall which becomes rather pleasant. But when you're just sitting in an absolutely plain wooden hall, it's unattractive and adds very little to the communal experience of hearing a concert with other people.'

A hall that sounds better after being painted a lighter colour or when there is something to look at shows how difficult it is to distinguish between perceptions about sound and other psychological responses – a fact which seems to have been given no attention in the past. Most work on acoustics has concerned the physical properties of sound and the physiology of the ear. The psychology of hearing – why one likes what one hears – is still a fairly new subject. Mike Barron of Cambridge University works in this field, and part of his research involves trying to measure subjective impressions – without which acoustics, he feels, cannot be truly scientific. This means giving quantifiable values to half-a-dozen basic words, such as 'timbre' and 'envelopment', by which he believes the entire acoustic spectrum can be summed up.

Meanwhile at Göttingen Univeristy in West Germany, Professor Manfred Schroeder has by-passed the problem of language and interpretation. In an ingenious piece of research, he transferred the concert-going experience into his laboratory by playing back a piece of music which had been played and re-recorded in twenty different auditoria around the world. Listeners were able to switch back and forth from one recording to another, and only had to say which of two halls at a time they preferred. This simple Better-Worse reply made it possible to avoid the difficulties of specialised vocabulary.

In the course of his work, Professor Schroeder studied the different acoustic signals received in each ear, and found that the more dissimilar they were, the better the hall was liked. The question then was how such differences in signal could be enhanced. The result of this work has been the development of a deeply-grooved ceiling structure which throws sound outwards towards the side walls, and from there to the ears, so that it is received in the brain as a secondary lateral reflection instead of as a frontal signal.

Research of this sort is what one looks for in the profession. Sadly, such research, or the application of such research, or even a working knowledge of such research, seems hard to come by, especially in this country. Acousticians tend to blame their lack of results on the other chap. They will tell you, for example, how difficult it is to get architects to take notice of acoustic tests. They will tell you how by the time a model of a proposed concert hall has been built and tested in miniature, the rest of the design process will have gone beyond the point at which any significant changes could be made. And that the chances are that there is not enough money to build a second model anyway if the first model shows that the design is unsatisfactory.

One's sympathies go out to acousticians. Of all the consultants who make up the building team, they are among the lowest in the pecking order. Their opinions are often disregarded and as a profession they have yet to prove their worth. On the other hand, acoustics is a very complex, inexact science, and it is only in recent years that its practitioners have begun to realise that while the path of sound can be plotted on paper with a straight edge and pencil, predicting the effect which that sound will have on the listener requires more subtle expertise.

The challenge which faces the acoustical profession is therefore dramatic; all their successes are yet to be achieved. But it feels as if the challenge is being spurned.

The halls with the best reputation among musicians and acousticians are without exception late nineteenth-century buildings – the Vienna Grosser Musikvereinssaal, the Amsterdam Concertgebouw, and the now-destroyed Leipzig Neues Gewandhaus, all of which are, or were, neo-classical coffered-ceiling, crystal-chandeliered, red-plush, gilt-encrusted, haut-bourgeois, over-decorated chunks of architectural wedding cake. Popular explanations for the success of these halls and others like them are unreliable in the extreme, especially among musicians. They like to tell each other that old halls are like violins – that they mature with age, which in turn has something to do with the quality of wood used in the construction of the stage. They also like to say that the empty space under the stage and the wall panelling resonate like the sound-box of a violin and that this helps rich, warm sounds to develop. In addition, it is thought that broken glass under the rostrum and gilt-encrusted angels on the ceiling give the music an added sharpness.

Many of these explanations are misinterpretations and some are positively wrong. That broken glass has been found under some stages testifies only to the drinking habits of a century or more of orchestras and stage crew, while the resonance of a violin in the production of a sound is quite different from the reverberation of a wooden floor or wall panel once the sound has been emitted. Sound is a form of energy which moves air, and can only be heard as long as it remains airborne. When the movement of air buffets something more solid, like wood, the energy is transformed into physical motion – the reverberation of the wood – and lost as sound. The sound, in other words, is not improved but killed. To keep a sound alive, therefore, it needs to be played in a setting where there is little to reverberate, or at least little which will reverberate at a frequency harmful to audible sound. Buildings made of stone, like cathedrals and churches, are a good example of settings in which sound may take a long time to decay. So the presence of wood has nothing to do with enhancing the quality of sound in the nineteenth-century halls. In fact, the very opposite applies. These halls are good because of their heavy masonry walls. The wood and plasterwork do not keep the sound resonating but absorb it, and thereby prevent echo.

Also important are the proportions of the old halls. Each, for all its ornamentation, is a simple rectangular box, about twice as long as it is wide, like a shoe-box. Because of this shape, sound is reflected off the side walls at just the right moment: not so soon that it prevents the slight blurring that gives richness and depth to the music, but, again, not so late that it creates an echo.

Until it was known why this type of hall was so good, there was no reason *not* to discard it, especially when new theories about the behaviour of sound were giving rise to new and apparently scientific architectural forms – wide halls with low ceilings, narrow halls with high ceilings, halls shaped like horseshoes and hexagons, and even halls shaped like lightbulbs.

In many cases, however, auditorium design has reflected a confusion rather than an understanding of how sound works. In the 1920s and 30s, new broadcasting and recording studios were lined with heavy insulation to soak up all the sound not directed to the microphone. The same principle, operating in reverse, was successfully applied to cinemas, in which sound was supplied by loudspeakers. But when it was incorporated into concert halls, the effects were disastrous.

Le Corbusier's unsuccessful competition entry for the League of Nations building in 1927 also made use of intelligent but misconceived ideas about how sound works. His wedge-shaped plan with its parabolic ceiling was in some ways analogous to the horn of an early gramophone, and operated on the same principle of directing pure sound from its source to its listener. But most music does not benefit from absolute clarity and while his design became an influential prototype for other architects, it was an acoustic failure.

Such has been the experience of the architectural profession during the scientific age that acousticians have begun to change their tune – none more so than Leo Beranek, who now seems a very chastened man of very different ambitions from his Philharmonic days. 'In the 1950s and 60s,' he says, 'one of our hopes was that we would be able to take halls of different shapes and sizes and make them all reasonably good acoustically. We now believe that if you want a truly good hall, you're going to have to copy another very good hall.' And that, by a process of reduction, means the Victorian shoe-box.

Vienna, Amsterdam and Leipzig were perfect settings for the music of the nineteenth century – music which needed to reverberate for just over two seconds for the individual notes to be heard as rich, harmonic chords. And since our concert repertoire is still largely nineteenth-century, the shoe-box model is still valid. And William Allen argues that it also offers the best acoustic compromise for other sorts of music. 'We would never work with anything else normally. The Festival Hall was a rectangular box. We worked there on the basis of better the devil you know than the devil you don't know.'

Theodore Schultz, however, who recently left Leo Beranek's practice after twenty years to go solo, believes that the shoe-box model has its limitations. 'Practically everybody if asked to name their favourite concert venue would say Vienna. The problem is that it works beautifully for a limited audience size, but as soon as you retain those shoe-box proportions but enlarge the hall to accommodate the audiences that are required today to support the hall and the salaries of the musicians, it fails. The sound takes too long to get from the side walls and back to the audience. So if we must – and we truly must – accommodate audiences of 2000 or 2500, then we've got to find some other way to provide those early sound reflections. If we could afford to rebuild Vienna, believe me, we'd do it. But we can't.'

The conventional way of testing a new design for a concert hall is to build a model of it and see how it performs. Some models are large enough to crawl inside; others are smaller. In all of them, the key is how to scale down the geometry of the building, the absorptive effects of the material in which the model is built, and the sounds used for testing. In the largest models, wood simulates brick and concrete, foam rubber simulates seating and human bodies, and speeded-up sound is injected into an auditorium flooded with nitrogen gas, which transmits sound more rapidly than air. Other techniques can involve the use of mirrored surfaces, smoke and laser beams, using light as a crude analogy for how sound travels.

Some methods are cheaper than others, some are easier to set up, but the whole process tends to be cumbersome and inaccurate. More important, physical models only allow you to examine one design at a time, which points to the main weakness of acoustics: that it is only capable of measuring, and not of predicting. This is perhaps why most of its successes have occurred in the refitting of existing buildings, such as the Maltings at Snape and the Buxton Opera House, rather than in the design of new ones.

But what are acousticians like those in Cambridge doing relying on wood and glue and foam rubber and laser beams anyway? The technology of research has gone far beyond such Heath Robinson affairs. Today, armed with a modest desk-top computer, designers could be building up digital, iterative designs, just as car manufacturers do, and making adjustments to their designs at the touch of a key if the echograms show that early reflections will arrive 50 milliseconds too late.

'This means that you can virtually build a concert hall in numbers and try it out,' says Rupert Taylor. 'You can have programmes that will track the path of a soundwave from its point of origin for quite a large number of reflections. You can predict what time the sound will arrive. And you can do that for every seat in the auditorium. Before long, we shall certainly be able to listen to sounds synthesised in a computer [model of a] concert hall. It will have shortcomings – so does everything – but it will enable us to save the disasters.'

Theodore Schultz, however, thinks it is not even worth pretending that acousticians can guarantee what a hall will sound like. 'I simply don't believe that what comes out of an acoustical model gets anywhere near the refinement that you're going to have to come to in the finished hall. In the automotive industry where millions of cars are built, you'd never dream of taking a car off the line without a thorough tune-up. Or when a chef creates a sauce, he begins with what he knows to be a basic recipe but then he tastes and seasons, tastes and seasons, and maybe throws it out. But in a one-off situation where you're spending $50 million or more on a design which has never been tried before and which is deliberately different in appearance from anything else, I think it's ridiculous to assume that you can put it on paper, build it, and fly with it and make everybody happy. The fact is, it takes a season, two seasons, three seasons to tune.'

This notion does violence to the idea of architecture as a predictive or a visionary art. It is high-priest architecture – an architecture which *sets* things right afterwards rather than *gets* things right first. The idea of refurbishment is the inspiration for such thinking. In other words, this is an architecture which has grown out of that one field where acousticians can claim to have scored successes. In vulgar terms it says: 'Build something, then worry about it once it's up.' What Theodore Schultz does is to build an approximation of what is required – perhaps too loose an approximation – and then treat it as a refit.

As a two-stage process, this draws out the length of his professional commitment to a project. Unfortunately there are halls in North America where money is simply not available to keep calling the high priest back to set things right. But the main criticism is with the intellectual loss of nerve which this way of working reflects. It is design which has given up.

Theodore Schultz tunes his buildings over several seasons, but some halls are designed to be retuned for every concert. 'Acoustic adjustability can be achieved in two ways,' explains Michael Forsyth, a Bristol architect and historian of concert halls. 'It can be achieved mechanically or electronically. If the variability is achieved mechanically, we start off with a building which has, one might say, the acoustics of the cave – very reverberant, very suitable for the music of Mahler, Richard Strauss, perhaps Brahms. A concert hall of that sort would have a reverberation time ideally of just over two seconds in the mid-frequencies when full up. Adjustability is achieved by introducing acoustic banners made of wool or some other absorbent material. This increases the amount of absorption in the hall and reduces the reverberation time. Halls have been built recently with a designed variability of from 1.5 to even 2.5 seconds. Nottingham is the very latest to be opened, and this is one of the few in Europe with mechanically variable acoustics.

'On the other hand, electronically assisted resonance, as it's known, is introduced into a building which one might regard as having the acoustics of the open air, where a hall is built first of all for speech – for great clarity of sound with a short reverberation time where it's dead like a recording studio. The hall then has a series of microphones and amplifiers and loudspeakers, and one can raise the reverberation time accordingly.'

It is a contest, then, between natural and artificial sound, each of which has an effect on the architectural form and the social conditions within the halls. To build large auditoria for natural sound, the orchestra has to be positioned centrally, or just off-centre, like the yolk in an egg. This can halve the maximum distance that sound has to travel to the most distant member of the audience. This is the way Ted Schultz designs, with a partly central rostrum surrounded by small plateaux of seats, known to architects as paddy fields or vineyard terraces. It is a solution first popularised by the German architect Hans Scharoun in 1963 in his Berlin Philharmonie.

Like its nineteenth-century predecessors, the Philharmonie's acoustic qualities were an accident of its aesthetic. Each plateau provides local, lateral reflections to groups of 100 to 200 people seated there. These reflections add detail to the overall presence of the sound. The plateaux also have political overtones. Each individual can identify with a small, local domain, while music-in-the-round brings him closer to the centre of things. Democracy, community and participation are the messages suggested by the building for those who want to read them. Herman Hertzberger's Muziekcentrum Vredenburg in Utrecht is one of many new halls in this genre which can be read in a similar way.

There are drawbacks to such designs, however, as the composer and conductor Pierre Boulez has discovered. 'The acoustic at Berlin is variable,' he says. 'It depends where you sit. If you are listening to a violin concerto, for instance, and you have the brass just in front of you, you hear this curtain of sound before you hear the soloist.'

There are visual problems as well. While the shoe-box hall can be taken in at a glance, the fragmented terraces of Berlin and similar auditoria can be difficult, and even disturbing, to grasp. The whole scene appears even more restless when the ceiling is hung with brightly coloured sound-absorbing banners, saucers and canopies. Theodore Schultz has provided such a setting at his Roy Thomson Hall in Toronto, the last building he worked on before leaving Bolt, Beranek, Newman. The Roy Thomson achieved a seating capacity of 2812 – 200 more than the very biggest of the big shoe-boxes, Sabine's Boston Symphony Hall, built in 1900. Mr Schultz can also make other claims for his hall: that no one sits more than 110 feet from the stage, unlike the 200-foot maximum at Boston.

But at what cost? Who, today, wants to sit in vast vulgar halls with crazy tilted saucers and garish multicoloured streamers listening to music invariably less reliable (because performance schedules mean that orchestras no longer have enough time to rehearse) than records, and less innovative (because economic constraints make lesser-known music unprofitable to perform), while being assaulted on all sides by coughing, sneezing, and the hourly chirrupping of a few dozen digitial wrist-watches, telling their owners – and everyone else in the vicinity – that it is now 8 o'clock, 9 o'clock, or, if they are very unlucky, 10 o'clock?

It is not just that it is now much more pleasant to get one's music informally, on the car radio or cycling to work or on a walk in the Pennines, with a performance by Klemperer of Mahler's 'Resurrection' personally delivered to your ears by courtesy of your headphones cassette. It is also that our musical standards are now so demanding that they can no longer be satisfied by live performances. Close-miking techniques used by recording engineers have led us to expect crystal-clear soloists against strong reverberant backgrounds, and such an effect is impossible to achieve under natural conditions. You would have to sit with one ear 12 inches from the performer and the other some 30 feet away in mid-air, and not even music critics are as big-headed as that.

These demands are not simply being made by audiences. They have been made by musicians for many years, as the acoustician Derek Sugden found when he was working on the Henry Wood Hall. 'They wanted it right for rehearsal first of all, and then right for recording, both of which can be very different. Most recording engineers like a very full reverberant sound because they're using close microphones and can deal with clarity. Whereas for rehearsal, if a conductor is going to get the balance right and hear the inner parts, then more clarity is needed. And these were nearly mutually exclusive requirements.'

Such problems are not unfamiliar to Pierre Boulez. 'I was with the Cleveland Orchestra in 1970, '71, and we were giving some tours in indoor stadiums. One evening we were playing *The Rite of Spring*, and the Cleveland were really playing their best and with quite a lot of volume. But one student came up to me later and said: "This evening was very disappointing, you know, the orchestra does not make any noise." And I said: "Aha! How can you judge that?" And he said: "Oh well, I've heard your recording." And I suppose that if you listen to a recording in a small room with two loudspeakers turned to full volume, and then hear an orchestra under normal conditions, there is a kind of disappointment between what you imagine the sound to be and the sound as you listen to it.'

The solution, however, would seem to be simple: to build concert halls which make sure of the second of the two options spelled out by Michael Forsyth – electronically assisted resonance. Hidden loudspeakers are already employed at the Royal Festival Hall which has 180 channels, but the most extreme case is the Kremlin Hall in Moscow. There the whole house is lined in a thick acoustic blanket. This deadens the live sound which is then reintroduced by loudspeakers located across the proscenium. These reproduce the locations of the instruments on stage, and provide the stereo effects. There are further speakers in the walls and ceilings, and these provide the reverberation. And then there is a speaker behind each seat. The reconstituted sound, picked up by twenty microphones hovering over the stage, is controlled by a Tone Master which, Orwellian though it sounds, can be very pleasing in practice. It also means that more than 6000 people – three times the regular number for a concert – can be accommodated, and provided with a perfect acoustical experience, and, if sheer numbers are the measure of a public event, a far more dramatic occasion.

Rupert Taylor is more committed than many of his collegues to the use of computers as a design tool, but he shares their reaction to the idea of electronics in the concert hall. 'They may be necessary to correct the shortcomings of existing halls,' he comments, 'and it does solve the problem and life goes on, but it's disastrous from the point of view of the acoustician. It's like going through life taking an aspirin every day.'

Andrew Porter of the *New Yorker* is more sanguine. 'I feel it to be wrong, but I can't actually say that it is wrong because I grew up with it in the Festival Hall without knowing it was there. We all admired so much the improvement of sound in the Festival Hall that when we learned too late that it was electronically assisted, we couldn't turn round and say: "This is all a fraud." '

Pierre Boulez is used to electronic sound in the music he composes and conducts, but even he will not warrant the use of loudspeakers in concert halls to give natural sound a boost. Even computerised music should be heard under natural conditions, he insists, though it is difficult to know quite how this could be achieved. The closest approximation to his ideal is the concert hall built for him at IRCAM, the Institut de Recherche et de Coordination Acoustique/Musique.

IRCAM is an organisation which luxuriates, as only a French institute can, in the earnest application of the principle of *reductio ad absurdum*, and which does so, naturally, in the name of *l'Art*. Where the Centre Pompidou, immediately to its north, parades its exterior guts like a vast lunar organ loft, IRCAM is so *reductio* as to be completely submerged underground. All that marks the entrance is a ticket kiosk for public concerts, and a pool filled with water-mobile sculptures by Alexander Calder which swirl and pirouette like figures in Bauhaus ballet, slooshing jets of water for the wind to catch and fling in the faces of the public – disconcerting for an arts centre, but preferable to paint pots.

A Metro-like staircase leads down to subterranean glass doors, beyond which, insulated from street noise by the blanket of water above, are the IRCAM laboratories where trails of computer wiring decorate the floor like staves from a John Cage manuscript. It gives the impression of visiting the wreck of a great ship: everywhere there are signs of life suspended – of apparatus in mid-experiment. In one room, a clarinet and a trumpet are locked in clamps on separate tables. They wear an expression of uncomprehending pain, like animals in a vivisection laboratory. They have motorised wind boxes attached so that the passage of air can be studied as it passes through them. But no one is actually studying; the scene is frozen in time. Meanwhile in the offices, clean-shaven lab *techniciens* pick seriously at the keys of IBM typewriters, and at their teeth. They are having to live through a perpetual insult: their computers are labelled in English. Surely this is not why President Georges Pompidou funded IRCAM.

IRCAM was set up by the French government in 1976 to fulfil some of the more eccentric musical prophecies of Erik Satie. To get from the reception desk to the office of its genius, Pierre Boulez, one climbs a spiral staircase and walks to the end of a metal cat-walk which runs past glass-fronted musical force-feeding pens. One of these belongs to *Monsieur le Directeur*. The cat-walk rattles at every step.

Pierre Boulez sits exactly where you would expect a composer of mid-twentieth-century experimental music to be sitting: hidden from view behind a metal filing cabinet with nothing on his desk but an empty in-tray and a pocket calculator. My arrival may well have interrupted him in the middle of calculating his next note, but he suddenly emerges from his hiding place, lit by a small table lamp. We sit down at a metal table which rattles, in metal seats with leather bases which groan and squeak. It is an environment rich in inspirational sounds – *les sons trouvés*.

Boulez has grown stouter and his face pudgier since he first became a favourite in London at the Proms in 1968. But he still conducts his conversation in the way he conducts an orchestra – chopping at the air with cupped hands.

'I don't want to give names but once I had to discuss with an acoustician this subject and it was really terrible because his idea was just to build a rectangular hall like the Vienna Musikverein, which he said was the only possible acoustic condition. He wouldn't accept that the orchestra and its needs had changed since Brahams. He would only have his rectangular hall with the orchestra set like in the nineteenth century. But you have some people who are more flexible and forward looking and they ask you: "What are the conditions, what do you need?" And what I need is a flexible stage so I can put an orchestra in different configurations, but without doing harm to the music. There have to be good fire exits, and instrument storage. And these problems are not always easy to reconcile with the acoustical constraints. So an acoustician has to look at all the conditions in which music is performed and not just at the acoustics. Some people are very open, but others are very closed to that.'

Strangely, Pierre Boulez's prescription for a modern concert hall does nothing to rule out the shoe-box. In fact, the experimental auditorium at IRCAM *is* a shoe-box, albeit small; it seats about 300. I visit it with one of the white-coated assistants. A young pianist and violinist are positioned on a low rostrum in the centre of the hall, surrounded on three sides by rows of canvas seats. They are practising a particularly anarchic rubato passage for a concert that evening. Whether they actually get it right does not seem to matter; what does matter is that the microphones get good pick-up. To this end, engineers are raising and lowering their mike booms, and conferring over their *talkie-walkies* with the control booth, where the crew seem to be watching non-stop multi-screen video re-runs of Pierre Boulez being interviewed.

The hall is a remarkable piece of design. It has a great slab of a ceiling which can be raised and lowered, giving you the unsettling impression of being trapped in a crusher in an automobile scrapyard. But its surfaces, and the surfaces of the walls, are not flat. They are honeycombed with recesses into which are set over a hundred three-sided revolving panels, each face of which has a different surface. The Ancient Greeks used similar revolving panels, known as *periaktoi*, with different paintings to signal to the audience whether the drama they were watching was tragic, comic, or satyric. Here, the *periaktoi* and the ceiling slab are also used to change the mood, but they do it by changing the acoustic identity of the room – the direction in which the sound is reflected, how much of it is absorbed, and the overall volume of the chamber. It is extremely elegantly done, and makes the banners and saucers of some of the larger halls seem even more clumsy and ill-thought-out.

These, then, seem to be the two extremes concert-hall design can take: intimate, acoustically flexible auditoria for natural sound, and the huge Muscovite arenas – veritable football stadiums of music. The problem with the latter is how to fill them. If Pierre Boulez will not accept the Kremlin Hall approach with its electronic reproduction, then it is unlikely that other more conservative musicians will. 'The solution,' says Boulez, 'is either to have gigantic orchestras of two hundred, and to multiply the number of violins and double the woodwinds and brass; or to make concerts in smaller halls. If you want good acoustics, that's a ratio that cannot be denied.'

To double the size of an orchestra or halve the size of the auditorium would mean doubling the cost of the tickets or halving the orchestra's salaries. Are such ideas feasible? Anthony Phillips is Concert Administrator for the South Bank complex in London, and his experience suggests that there is an irreconcilable clash between acoustic and economic demands. 'Bearing in mind that most concerts take place in some sort of subsidised context,' he says, 'the number of seats I would say for economic viability seems to be around 2700, 2800, possibly as many as 3000. Whereas the nicest, warmest, cleanest natural sound seems to come from halls of about 1500, maybe up to 1800.

'The majority of programmes that are in our programme at the moment, done by a major London orchestra with a fine conductor and an international soloist, will produce at 100 per cent of capacity around £15,000 in the Festival Hall. Immediately you have to remove from that VAT at 15 per cent which will knock it down to £13,000. Additionally, the economics of selling involve some kind of discounting – reductions for subscription tickets – and maybe all the seats aren't sold. So one can work on a 70 per cent financial taking which will bring it down to £9000 or £10,000. Whereas the real cost of putting on an orchestral performance in the Festival Hall must be about £15,000. So there's a gap of about £6000 which is why the London Orchestral Board current subsidy is now, not without reason, £6000.'

Even when a popular work is performed to a capacity audience by a first-rate orchestra then, a top-class medium-to-large-sized concert hall will not pay its way. That suggests that since the costs of orchestras, soloists, concert-hall staff, heating, lighting and maintenance are going to be much the same in a 3000-seat auditorium as in a 2000 seater, one might as well build the larger hall and maximise box-office takings whenever possible. But Andrew Porter disagrees.

'I think there must be a fallacy in the argument. The composer Gian-Carlo Menotti once proposed what he called Menotti's law, which was simply that the larger the house, the larger the subsidy it requires. He said it had never been disproved, and in my experience it has never been disproved. When Sadler's Wells Opera moved from Sadler's Wells and became the English National Opera at the larger Coliseum, at once its budget had to get much bigger, and similarly its subsidies.

'I also think the size of a concert hall actually dictates the sort of music which is heard by the public, and that's not healthy because it's so concentrated on the narrow part of the repertory which suits large concert halls – music from the mid-nineteenth century to the early twentieth century. I'd like to think that the public really wants to hear Mozart played by a Mozart-sized orchestra, a Mozart-in-volume orchestra. That kind of performance is simply lost in a concert hall that seats 3000 people' – visually as well as acoustically, as anyone knows who has sat in the back row of the Festival Hall or up in the gallery at the Albert Hall.

This leaves the acoustical consultant in a double bind. The small auditorium is too small to be economically viable; the large one is too big. The small one will not cover its running costs even if it is always full to capacity; the large one will not cover its costs because it cannot be adequately or regularly filled, either with people or with sound. So even without going into the question of how competent the profession may be, it is possible to say in advance that the acoustician is going to fail, for reasons which include the economics of ticket selling, the physical properties of sound, and the social trends of audiences.

Concert-hall managers could always take a leaf out of the opera houses' book and put on repeats of the same concert. Or they could offer season tickets. Or they could give away tickets as an incentive. Or they could hold more subscription concerts. Or hang advertising banners from the ceiling. Or ask the musicians to wear sponsorship T-shirts like footballers. Or. . . .

Life does not need to be so difficult. Some efforts are counter-productive. Some problems have no solution. If concert-hall managers continue to rely on the standard repertoire of over-familiar concert classics, they will continue to bore their audiences away. If they take a risk and put on new or unfamiliar music, they will scare them away. It is a vicious circle, in the middle of which stands the acoustician – the scapegoat of the piece, being asked to solve a problem that cannot be solved. It would be a lot easier to declare the concert hall and all its attendant worries over and defunct. Since the record rather than the performance has now become the standard unit of measure in music, the live perform-ance has become in turn an eccentricity which is unrepresentative of what the public now takes to be its musical truths. Under such circumstances, it is time to cry: *Vive le hi-fi! Vive le radio! Vive le Walkman!*